MW01296450

Zechariah: Israel and Her Coming King

Zechariah: Israel and Her Coming King

Dr. David Schnittger, President
Southwest Prophecy Ministries

© 2017 Dr. David Schnittger
All rights reserved.

ISBN-13: 9781974266890
ISBN-10: 1974266893

Table of Contents

Foreword

§

ZECHARIAH IS A MINOR PROPHET with a major message! This book has more prophecies concerning Christ than any other of the Minor Prophets. There are multiple detailed prophecies concerning the first advent of Christ: His triumphal entry, His betrayal, His sufferings and the dispersion of Israel. Each one was fulfilled with absolute accuracy! There are even more prophecies concerning His second advent: His return to the Mount of Olives, the protection of a Jewish remnant, His appearance to the Jews in Petra in a great day of national atonement, resulting in their spiritual and material restoration, His building of the Millennial Temple, and the nature of worship in the Millennium. I believe that each one of these prophecies will likewise be fulfilled with absolute accuracy! This study will increase your confidence in the sure Word of prophecy as well as your love for Christ's return.

Preface

§

*And his feet shall stand in that day upon the mount of Olives,
which is before Jerusalem on the east, and the mount of Olives shall
cleave in the midst thereof toward the east and toward the west,
and there shall be a very great valley; and half of the mountain
shall remove toward the north, and half of it toward the south.*

(KJV throughout)
Zechariah 14:4

The prophetic book of Zechariah has long been this author's favorite book in the section of the Old Testament known as "The Minor Prophets." The purpose of writing this book is threefold. The first reason is to demonstrate that the book is not *diminutive*. Though the brief length of the book justifies its inclusion in the twelve books known as "The Minor Prophets," it is not minor in terms of its importance. It is one of the most important books in the Old Testament in terms of its Christology and its eschatology. We learn much in Zechariah about the first and second comings of Christ and the establishment of His earthly millennial kingdom. We also learn much regarding the future of God's covenant nation, Israel.

The second reason I wrote this book is to demonstrate that Zechariah is not *difficult*. Some Bible interpreters make the book difficult because they utilize an unnatural approach to interpreting it. They say that Zechariah should be interpreted metaphorically, allegorically, or "spiritually." They try to interject and impose the "church" upon the text, although the church is nowhere to be seen in Zechariah. In fact, according to the Apostle Paul, the church is nowhere to be found in the entire Old Testament (cf. Ephesians 3:1-6).

The Apostle Paul tells us that "all scripture is . . . profitable . . ." (2 Timothy 3:16). By understanding Zechariah according to the normal rules of literary interpretation, we can derive great insight and profit from its clear teachings. For example, we can appreciate the fact that all the prophecies regarding Christ's first coming described in Zechariah were fulfilled literally and with great specificity. Thus we can anticipate that all the prophecies pertaining to Christ's second coming will also be fulfilled in a literal manner. There is spiritual profit to be derived from this certainty!

The third reason I wrote this book is to dispel the notion that Zechariah is a *discouraging* book. Though there is information pertaining to suffering and judgment in the book, the overall tone is that of encouragement. In like fashion, sometimes we are prone to become discouraged as we see Satan's "new world order" moving forward in ways that seem unstoppable. This is merely a temporary illusion. In reality, it is not Satan's "new world order" that is unstoppable; it is Christ's "New World Order" that is unstoppable. The book of Zechariah reminds us that, for Christians, we are not only on the right side of history, but we are also on the *winning* side of history!

David P. Schnittger

CHAPTER 1
Introduction to Zechariah

§

As STATED IN THE PREFACE there are some Bible interpreters who teach that the prophetic passages in the book of Zechariah cannot be interpreted literally. Amillennialists are one such group. Amillennialists (otherwise known as "realized millennialists") believe that the Bible does not predict a literal rule of Christ on earth before the last judgment. Walter Elwell describes the Amillennial viewpoint as follows:

> According to this outlook there will be a continuous development of good and evil in the world until the second coming of Christ, then the dead shall be raised and the judgment conducted. Amillennialists believe that the kingdom of God is now present in the world as the victorious Christ rules his church through the Word and the Spirit. They feel that the future, glorious, and perfect kingdom refers to the new earth and life in heaven. Thus Revelation 20 is a description of the souls of dead believers reigning with Christ in heaven.[1]

---

1 W. Elwell, *Evangelical Dictionary of Theology.* (Grand Rapids: Baker Book House, 1984), 715.

To give you an example of how this affects one's interpretation of Zechariah, Marten Woudstra, an Amillennial author, interprets Zechariah 14 this way:

> From the mixed character of the imagery employed, referring now to cataclysmic upheavals, now to regular pilgrimages to Jerusalem, it seems to this writer that no such literal interpretation of the passages is intended. The prophecy has in view various aspects of the gospel age with particular emphasis on its conclusion.[2]

In other words, to the Amillennialist, the prophecies of Zechariah should be interpreted metaphorically, allegorically, or "spiritually" rather than literally. The prophecies in Zechariah, according to the Amillennial school of interpretation, refer to the Church Age, not to a literal future and earthly millennial kingdom. I like the honesty of a famous Amillennialist, Martin Luther, as he tried to interpret Zechariah 14. Luther said, "Here in this chapter, I give up. For I am not sure what the prophet is talking about."[3] If we take a non-literal approach to Zechariah, can we hope to be more successful in understanding it than Martin Luther, who had a Ph.D. in theology and was the "Father of the Protestant Reformation"?

Another non-literal interpretation of the book of Zechariah is the preterist (past) view. That is the interpretation of the prophetic portions of Zechariah that asserts that Zechariah is a symbolic assortment of prophecies describing the destruction of Jerusalem in A.D. 70, together

---

2 M. Woudstra, *The Biblical Expositor*, Vol. 2 (Philadelphia: A.J. Holman Co., 1960), 377-378.

3 M. Luther, "Lectures on Zechariah. The German Text, 1527" in *Luther's Works*, Vol. 20: *Lectures on the Minor Prophets III: Zechariah* (ed. Hilton c. Oswald; Saint Louis: Concordia, 1973), 337.

with the spread of the gospel throughout the Church Age thereafter. In other words, prophecies concerning the second coming of Christ have been fulfilled in the past.[4]

As we look at the *fulfilled* prophecies of Zechariah that were *literally fulfilled* in the first coming of Christ, this gives us the indication that the inspired prophet expected the *literal fulfillment* of that which is yet to come. We should emerge from this study with great confidence that what God has predicted will surely and literally come to pass in real time and real space and real soon! Before we actually get into the text of Zechariah, let's consider some introductory issues.

HISTORICAL BACKGROUND

Zechariah's prophetic ministry took place in the time of Judah's restoration from the Babylonian captivity, in what is known as the post-exilic period. When Jeremiah's prophesied 70 period of captivity was completed (606-536 B.C.), God influenced Cyrus, the Persian king, to allow the Hebrews to return to their homeland and rebuild their temple. Babylon fell to Cyrus in 539 B.C. Shortly thereafter, Cyrus issued an edict that permitted the Hebrew remnant to return to Judah and rebuild her temple. We read in Ezra 1:1-4:

> Now in the first year of Cyrus king of Persia, that the word of the LORD stirred up the spirit of Cyrus king of Persia, that he made a proclamation through all his kingdom, and put it also in writing, saying, Thus saith Cyrus king of Persia, The LORD God of heaven hath given me all the kingdoms of the earth; and he had charged me to build him an house at Jerusalem, which is in Judah. Who is there among you of all his people? His God be with him, and let him go up to Jerusalem, which is

---

4 G.N. M. Collins, *The New Bible Commentary*, (Grand Rapids: Eerdmans, 1954), 761-763.

in Judah, and build the house of the LORD God of Israel, (he is the God,) which is in Jerusalem. And whosoever remaineth in any place where he sojourneth, let the men of his place help him with silver, and with gold, and with goods, and with beasts, beside the freewill offering for the house of God that is in Jerusalem.

It is noteworthy that a heathen emperor, Cyrus the Great, had somehow come to recognize the fact that the God of the Hebrews was actually the God of creation. It may be that the prophet Daniel, who was Cyrus' prime minister, led him to this conviction.

As Ezra indicates, this decree was in fulfillment of ". . . the word of the LORD by the mouth of Jeremiah . . ." This promise is recorded in Jeremiah 29:10: "For thus saith the Lord, That after seventy years be accomplished at Babylon I will visit you, and perform my good word toward you, in causing you to return to this place."

In the nineteenth century, the archaeological discovery of the "Cyrus cylinder" confirms the historicity of the decree of Cyrus. This cylinder, inscribed in Babylonian cuneiform in the name of King Cyrus the Great, was found in 1879 in present-day Iraq by Mr. Hormuzd Rassam at Babylon, and dates back to the sixth century B.C. This cylinder describes not only the capture of Babylon, but also Cyrus' permission for the people captured by the Babylonians to return to their homelands. Although the Hebrews are not mentioned by name, the text refers to the repatriation of deported people which would

THE CYRUS CYLINDER

certainly include the Hebrews. Scholars have linked one particular passage from the cylinder to the decree of Cyrus:

> From . . . Assur and [from] Susa, Agade, Esnunna, Zamban, Meturnu, Der, as far as the region of Gutium, the sacred centers on the other side of the Tigris, whose sanctuaries had been abandoned for a long time, I returned the images of the gods, who had resided there [i.e., in Babylon], to their places and I let them dwell in eternal abodes. **I gathered all their inhabitants and returned to them their dwellings** (emphasis added).[5]

Consequent to the decree of Cyrus a large group did return in 538-537 B.C. under the civil leadership of Zerubbabel, the governor, and the religious leadership of Joshua, the high priest. This group included a congregation of 42,360, a staff of 7,337 servants and maids, plus 200 singers (Ezra 2:64-66). This group completed the foundation of the temple early in 536 B.C. (Ezra 3:8-13), but several obstacles arose that slowed and finally halted the construction (Ezra 4:1-5, 24). The construction resumed in 520 B.C., and the temple was finished in 516 B.C.

The historical circumstances and conditions that Zechariah ministered under were, in general, those of Haggai's time, since their labors were contemporary. Thus, the immediate historical background for Zechariah's ministry began with Cyrus, who captured Babylon in 539 B.C. and concluded with the completion of the second temple (516 B.C.).

Author

Zechariah was not only a prophet but also a priest. He was born in Babylon and was among those who returned to Judah in 538-537 B.C.

---

5 T.G. Pinches, "Cyrus" *International Standard Bible Encyclopedia.* (Grand Rapids: Eerdmans, 1939) II: 775.

under the leadership of Zerubbabel and Joshua (Nehemiah 12:4). At a later time, when Joiakim was high priest, Zechariah apparently succeeded his grandfather Iddo (Zech 1:1, 7) as head of that priestly family (Neh 12:10-16). Since it was the grandson (Zechariah) who in this instance succeeded his grandfather (Iddo), it has been conjectured that the father (Berekiah – Zech 1:1, 7) died at an early age, before he could succeed to family headship.

Though a contemporary of Haggai, Zechariah continued his ministry long after him (Neh 12:10-16). Considering his young age in the early period of his ministry (he is referred to as a "young man" in Zechariah 2:4), it is possible that Zechariah continued his ministry into the reign of Artaxerxes I (465-424 B.C.).

The prophet's name itself has theological significance. It means "Yahweh remembers." In the context of the book of Zechariah, it denotes that Yahweh remembers his covenant promises to Israel and acts to fulfill them. In the book of Zechariah, God's promised deliverance from Babylonian captivity, including a restored theocratic community and a functioning temple, would lead to even grander prophecies of the salvation and restoration to come through the Messiah.

DATE

The dates of Zechariah's writings may be correlated with those of Ezra and Haggai and with the following historical events:

- The resumption of the building of the temple (Ezra 5:2) – September 520 B.C.
- The beginning of Zechariah's preaching – October/November 520 B.C.
- Zechariah's eight night visions (Zech 1:7-6:8) – February 519 B.C.

- Joshua's crowning as Judah's high priest (Zech 6:9-15) – February 519 B.C.
- Urging of repentance, promise of blessings (Zech 8-9) – December 518 B.C.
- Dedication of the temple (Ezra 6:15-18) – March 516 B.C.
- Zechariah's final prophecy (Zech 9-14) – After 480 B.C.

PLACE OF COMPOSITION

At the time of his prophesying and writing, Zechariah was clearly back in Judah, and his ministry was to the returned exiles. Zechariah is mentioned by name in Nehemiah 12 as being among the priests and Levites that went up with Zerubbabel to Judah. Nehemiah 12:1, 16 states: "Now these are the priests and the Levites that went up with Zerubbabel . . . Of Iddo, Zechariah . . ."

OCCASION AND PURPOSE

The occasion of the book is the return of the approximately fifty thousand former exiles to Jerusalem and the nearby Judean towns in 538-537 B.C. with high hopes of resettling the land and rebuilding the temple (Ezra 2). Upon returning to Judah, they immediately set up the altar of burnt offering (Ezra 3:1-6). They resumed worship and restored the sacrificial ritual that had been suspended during the seventy years of exile in Babylonia. The people then laid the foundation of the temple (536 B.C.), but their efforts soon met with opposition in various forms as stated in Ezra 4:1-5:

> Now when the adversaries or Judah and Benjamin heard that the children of the captivity builded the temple unto the LORD God of Israel; Then they came to Zerubbabel, and to the chief of the fathers, and said unto them, Let us build with you: for we

seek your God, as ye do; and we do sacrifice unto him since the days of Esarhaddon king of Assur, which brought us up hither. But Zerubbabel, and Jeshua, and the rest of the chief of the fathers of Israel, said unto them, Ye have nothing to do with us to build an house unto our God; but we ourselves together will build unto the LORD God of Israel, as king Cyrus the king of Persia hath commanded us. Then the people of the land weakened the hands of the people of Judah, and troubled them in building, And hired counselors against them, to frustrate their purpose, all the days of Cyrus, king of Persia, until the reign of Darius king of Persia.

Therefore, the reconstruction of what became known as "Zerubbabel's Temple" ground to a halt and did not begin again until 520 B.C. Ezra 4:24 states: "Then ceased the work of the house of God which is at Jerusalem. So it ceased unto the second year of the reign of Darius king of Persia." The chief purpose of the book of Zechariah, therefore, was to rebuke the people and encourage them to complete the rebuilding of the temple. Zechariah was also clearly interested in the spiritual renewal of the Hebrews as well. This is demonstrated in Zechariah 1:3: ". . . Thus saith the LORD of hosts; Turn ye unto me, saith the LORD of hosts, and I will turn unto you . . ." The Lord asked the Hebrews to return to Him; then He would return to them, and His promises to them would continue to be fulfilled.

THEOLOGICAL VALUES

George Robinson says in regard to the book of Zechariah: "Few books of the OT are as difficult of interpretation as the book of Zechariah; no other book is as Messianic . . . In the present writer's judgment, his

book is the most Messianic the must truly apocalyptic and eschatological of all the writings of the OT.[6]

Levy adds to the prophetic significance of Zechariah by stating:

There are two reasons why Christians should be interested in
Zechariah. One is because of the clear prophecies concerning
Jesus Christ's person and ministry that were fulfilled in the New
Testament. The Messianic prophecies in the book of Zechariah
are second only to those in Isaiah. The other reason is how the
prophecies concerning end-times events relate to Israel, the city
of Jerusalem, the Second Coming of Jesus Christ, and worship
in the Millennial Kingdom. The book of Zechariah is not only
the longest of the Minor Prophets but also the most frequently
quoted in the New Testament.[7]

Zechariah predicted Christ's coming in lowliness (6:12); His humanity (6:12); His rejection and betrayal for thirty pieces of silver (11:12,
13); His being struck by the sword of the Lord (13:7); His deity (3:4;
13:7a); His priesthood (6:13); and His kingship (6:13; 9:9; 14:9, 16). As
for the apocalyptic and eschatological aspects of his writing, Zechariah
predicted Christ's second coming in glory (14:4); His building of the
LORD's temple (6:12, 13); His reign (9:10, 14); and His establishment
of enduring peace and prosperity (3:20; 9:9-12). He also predicted the
final siege of Jerusalem (12:1-3; 14:1, 2); the initial victory of Israel's
enemies (14:2); the Lord's defense of Jerusalem (14:3, 4); the judgment

---

6 G. Robinson, *The International Standard Bible Encyclopedia* (Grand Rapids: Eerdmans,
1939), V: 3136.

7 David Levy, *Zechariah: Israel's Prophetic Future and the Coming Apocalypse*
(Bellmawr, NJ: The Friends of Israel Gospel Ministry, Inc., 2011), 6.

on the nations (12:9; 14:3); the topographical changes in Israel (14:4, 5); the celebration of the Feast of Tabernacles in the Messianic Kingdom Age (14:16-19); and the ultimate holiness of Jerusalem and her people. Finally, the book as a whole teaches the sovereignty of God in history, over men and nations – past, present and future.

Literary Form and Hermeneutics

The book of Zechariah is primarily a mixture of exhortation (e.g. a call to repentance, 1:2-6); prophetic visions (1:7-6:8); and judgment and salvation oracles (chapters 9-14). The prophetic visions of 1:7-6:8 are apocalyptic literature, which may be defined as "symbolic, visionary prophetic literature, composed during oppressive conditions consisting of visions whose events are recorded exactly as they were seen by the author and explained through a divine interpreter and whose theological content is primarily eschatological."[8]

Apocalyptic literature is basically meant to encourage the people of God. When the apocalyptic section of Zechariah (1:7-6:8) is added to the salvation oracles in chapters nine through fourteen, it becomes clear that the dominant emphasis of the book is encouragement to God's people because of their glorious future. A special problem created by the apocalyptic visions (1:7-6:8) and by the judgment and deliverance oracles (chs. 9-14) is how they are to be handled interpretively. This author's view is that Zechariah is to be interpreted according to the literal-grammatical-historical method.

"Literal" means that we take the words for what they mean in their normal or plain sense. "Grammatical" means that we follow the normal grammatical rules of interpreting literature. "Historical" means that we seek with diligence to determine the historical background

---

8 R. Alexander, "Hermeneutics of Old Testament Apocalyptic Literature." (Th.D. dissertation, Dallas Theological Seminary, 1968), 45.

and context before rendering an interpretation. As applied to the book of Zechariah, the employment of the literal-grammatical-historical method basically means that even in prophetic literature one should interpret the text literally or normally unless the context of the book itself or the Bible elsewhere clearly suggests otherwise. Obviously since certain literary genres – such as apocalyptic literature and poetry in general – abound in types, symbols, and other figures of speech, much of this type of literature must be interpreted typologically, symbolically and figuratively. Fortunately, in most instances the text itself or the biblical context furnishes the interpretation of such language.[9]

STRUCTURE AND THEMES

A. *Structure*: While Zechariah may be divided into two parts (chs. 1-8 and chs. 9-14), it likewise falls rather naturally into five major divisions:

- 1:1-6 – Introduction and call to repentance;
- 1:7-6:8 – Eight night visions;
- 6:9-15 – The symbolic crowning of Joshua the high priest;
- Chapters 7-8 – The question about fasting;
- Chapters 9-14 – Two prophetic oracles (9-11 and 12-14)

B. *Themes*: The central theme of Zechariah is encouragement – primarily encouragement to complete the rebuilding of the temple. Various means are used to accomplish this end and these function as subthemes. For example, great stress is laid on the coming of the Messiah and His overthrow of all anti-kingdom

---

9 Mark Esposito, "The Literal Grammatical Historical Method" www.endtimes. org/grammat.html

forces so that Christ's millennial kingdom can be finally and fully established on earth.

CANONICITY AND VALUE

The second division of the Hebrew canon (the Prophets) closes with the Twelve Minor Prophets, and Zechariah is placed next to last on the list. Neither Jews nor Christians have ever seriously challenged its right to be in the canon. Its value is demonstrated by the frequency with which the New Testament quotes it and alludes to it. For example, in Zechariah 13:7 we read:

> Awake, O sword, against my shepherd, and against the man that is my fellow, saith the LORD of hosts: smite the shepherd, and the sheep shall be scattered: and I will turn mine hand upon the little ones.

This verse is quoted by Jesus in Mark 14:27:

> And Jesus saith unto them, All ye shall be offended because of me this night: for it is written, I will smite the shepherd, and the sheep shall be scattered.

Additionally, there are a multitude of verses in Zechariah that, while not being directly quoted in the New Testament, are directly fulfilled in the New Testament. For example, Zechariah 11:12, 13 states:

> And I said unto them, if ye think good, give me my price; and if not, forbear. So they weighed for my price thirty pieces of silver. And the Lord said unto me, Cast it unto the potter – a lordly

price that I was prized of them. And I took the thirty pieces of silver, and cast them to the potter in the house of the Lord.

Though not quoted in the New Testament, the remarkable accuracy and detail of this prophecy is shown not only by the disclosure of the exact amount of "blood money" given, but also by the fact that it would be thrown down in the house of the Lord by the conscience-stricken Judas, and that the money would be used to purchase the potter's field to bury Judas. This is revealed in Matthew 27:5-7:

And he cast down the pieces of silver in the temple, and departed, and went and hanged himself. And the chief priests took the silver pieces, and said, It is not lawful for to put them into the treasury, because it is the price of blood. And they took counsel, and bought with them the potter's field, to bury strangers.

With these introductory issues in hand, in the next chapter we will give, in great detail, an overview of the topic of Israel in the Church Age.[10]

---

10 Introductory issues resource: K.L. Barker, "Zechariah" *The Expositor's Bible Commentary* (Grand Rapids: Zondervan, 1985) Vol. 7: 595-599.

CHAPTER 2

Israel in The Church Age

§

IN THIS CHAPTER WE ARE going to look at what God's Word says pertaining to Israel in the church age. Let me begin by defining terms: By "Israel" I am referring to the "children of promise," which are the children of Abraham, Isaac and Jacob. I am not just referring to the children of Abraham, as that would include, for example, Ishmael, the father of the Ishmaelites, whose descendants have been bitter enemies of Israel for millennia. By "Israel" I am referring to, not only the "children of promise" (i.e., ethnic Israel), but also the modern nation-state of Israel, founded in 1948. The modern Jewish state is partly occupied by the "children of promise." I believe the promises made to "Israel" pertain only to the children of Abraham, Isaac and Jacob, whether or not they are presently residing in the nation of Israel. There are several features that need to be covered to deal adequately with the subject, "Israel in the Church age."

ISRAEL'S REJECTION OF MESSIAH IN THE GOSPELS

The four gospels all deal in great detail with the narrative of the Jew's rejection of Christ (cf. Mt 15:6-14; Lk 23:17-23; Jo 18:39, 40). For example, we read in Matthew 27:22-25:

> Pilate saith unto them, What shall I do then with Jesus which is called Christ? They (the chief priest, elders and the multitude – v 20) all say unto him, Let him be crucified. And the

governor said, Why, what evil hath he done? But they cried out the more saying, Let him be crucified. When Pilate saw that he could prevail nothing, but that rather a tumult was made, he took water, and washed his hands before the multitude, saying, I am innocent of the blood of this just person: see ye to it. Then answered all the people (the Jews), and said, His blood be on us, and on our children.

ISRAEL'S REJECTION OF MESSIAH IN THE ACTS PERIOD

The apostles made no secret in their preaching that the Jews were responsible for the crucifixion of Jesus, even though the execution was carried out by the Roman government. Peter, for example, declared in his sermon on the Day of Pentecost in Acts 2:22-24:

Ye men of Israel, hear these words: Jesus of Nazareth, a man approved of God among you by miracles and wonders and signs, which God did by him in the midst of you, as ye yourselves also know: Him, being delivered by the determinate counsel and foreknowledge of God, ye have taken, and by wicked hands have crucified and slain:

This pattern of Jewish rejection of their Messiah continued throughout the book of Acts. During the Acts period, the gospel was ". . . to the Jew first, and also to the Greek" (Ro 1:16). The apostles practiced this Jewish gospel priority throughout the Acts period (A.D. 33-63). We see this pattern, for example, with Paul and Barnabas in their ministry in Antioch in Pisidia, as recorded in Acts 13:44-46:

And the next Sabbath day came almost the whole city together to hear the word of God. But when the Jews saw the multitudes, they were filled with envy, and spake against those things which were spoken by Paul, contradicting and blaspheming and said, It was necessary that the word of God should **first** have been spoken to you: but seeing ye put it from you, and judge yourselves unworthy of everlasting life, lo, **we turn to the Gentiles.** (emphasis added)

This pattern of Jewish gospel priority continued throughout the book of Acts. The reoffer of the gospel and the kingdom to Israel came to a climax in Acts 28. It was during Paul's first Roman imprisonment that ". . . Paul called the chief of the Jews together . . ." (v 17) where ". . . he expounded and testified the kingdom of God, persuading them concerning Jesus, both out of the law of Moses, and *out of* the prophets, from morning till evening" (v 23). Paul's witness met with mixed reviews: "And some believed the things which were spoken, and some believed not. And when they agreed not among themselves they departed . . ." (v 24, 25a). This was the Jews' final opportunity *as a nation* to receive Christ as their Messiah during the church age, as Paul proceeds to pronounce the curse of Isaiah 6:9, 10 upon unbelieving Israel (Acts 28:25b-28):

> . . . after that Paul had spoken one word, Well spake the Holy Ghost by Esaiah the prophet unto our father, Saying, Go unto this people, and say, Hearing ye shall hear, and shall not understand; and seeing ye shall see, and not perceive: For the heart of this people is waxed gross, and their ears are dull of hearing, and their eyes have they closed; lest they should see with their eyes, and hear with their ears, and understand with their heart, and should be converted and I should heal them. Be it known therefore unto you, that the salvation of God is sent unto the Gentiles, and *that* they will hear it.

During the entirety of the Acts period, God gave Israel an extended "second chance" to repent and receive Christ as their promised Messiah with the prospect of the kingdom of heaven – the second coming/ Millennium. Respected Bible scholar, J. Sidlow Baxter, concurs with this view.[11] With their conclusive rejection at the end of the book of Acts, Israel is set aside in unbelief and the gospel is sent to the gentiles. This conclusive rejection is consequently met with devastating judgment that took place in A.D. 68-70 with the siege of Jerusalem, resulting in massive slaughter of the Jews and their long-term dispersion. Jesus spoke to the unbelieving Jews in Jerusalem about this judgment as recorded in Luke 19:42-44:

> If thou hadst known, even thou, at least in this thy day, the things which belong unto thy peace! But now they are hid from thine eyes. For the days shall come upon thee, that thine enemies shall cast a trench about thee, and compass thee round, and keep thee in on every side, And shall lay thee even with the ground, and thy children within thee; and they shall not leave in thee one stone upon another; because thou knewest not the time of thy visitation.

ISRAEL'S CURRENT SPIRITUAL STATE

What does God's Word say about Israel during the present church age? Paul addresses the subject of God's plan for Israel in Romans 9-11. In

---

11 "The renewed offer of the kingdom of heaven to Israel has been made over a period of thirty years, first to the Jews of the homeland, then to the Jews of the Dispersion throughout the Roman world, and finally to the Jews at the imperial city. With that message of the re-offered kingdom there has been coupled the wonderful Saviourhood of the Messiah, Jesus, through His Calvary sacrifice, and the fact of His Resurrection. But in general the Jewish attitude has everywhere been unbelieving and hostile." J. Sidlow Baxter, *Explore the Book* (London: Marshall, Morgan & Scott, Ltd. 1955), 6:34, 35.

this section of Romans, Paul deals with Israel's past, Israel's present and Israel's future.[12] In regard to Israel's present state, Paul deals with the unbelief of Israel and the responsibility of Israel. In sum, Israel's rejection of Messiah was due to their reliance on law-keeping rather than faith. Paul declares in Romans 9:31, 32:

> But Israel, which followed after the law of righteousness, hath not attained to the law of righteousness. Wherefore? Because they sought it not by faith, but as it were by the works of the law. For they stumbled at that stumbling-stone (Christ);

As a result of that, Israel as a nation has been set aside in unbelief; yet the elect of Israel are being saved in the church age. Paul makes that clear in Romans 11:7: "What then? Israel hath not obtained that which he seeketh for; but the election hath obtained it, and the rest were blinded." Paul discloses how long this "partial blindness" of Israel will be in Romans 11:25:

> For I would not, brethren, that ye should be ignorant of this mystery, lest ye should be wise in your own conceits; that blindness in part is happened to Israel, until the fullness of the Gentiles be come in.

I believe the "fullness of the Gentiles" has to do with the church age and the Tribulation, culminating in the second coming of Christ. So, while ethnic Jews nationally are not presently "God's people," the Bible predicts that a remnant will be saved at the end of the tribulation. The

---

12 For an extensive treatment of Romans 9-11, the author recommends Steven A. Kreloff, *God's Plan for Israel* (Neptune, NJ: Loizeaux, 1995).

similarity of language between Zechariah and Hosea is noteworthy: Zechariah 13:8, 9 reads:

> In the whole land (Israel), declares the Lord, two-thirds will be struck down and perish; yet one-third will be left in it. This third I will bring into the fire; I will refine them like silver and test them like gold. They will call on my name and I will answer them; I will say, "They are my people," and they will say, "The LORD is our God."

How then does God look at Israel today? Paul quotes from Hosea 2:10 and 2:23 in Romans 9:25 to answer that question:

> As he saith also in Osee (Hosea), I will call them my people, which were not people; and her beloved, which was not beloved. And it shall come to pass, that in the place where it was said unto them, Ye are not my people; there shall they be called the children of the living God.

Let me quote directly from Hosea 1:10 to get the full impact of the consequences of Israel's unbelief: "Then said *God*, Call his name Lo-ammi: for ye *are* not my people and I will not be your *God*." In context, the Lord is naming Gomer's second son "Lo-ammi," meaning "Not my people." This was prophetic of the coming exile of Israel to Assyria, which took place in 722 B.C. This same prophecy from Hosea is quoted by Paul in Romans 9:25 and applied to Judah's then future exile and dispersion by the Romans in A.D. 70.

It is important that we reflect God's view of ethnic Israel in the church age. Some, in their zeal to defend the Jewish nation, give the impression that Israel can do no wrong, and that it is our Christian duty to support their every action as a nation. God Himself does not meet that standard, as the Word of God declares that Israel is "Lo-ammi" and that they "pollute my holy name." Israel is back in the land in *unbelief.* We must be patient for God to take Israel "to the woodshed" during the time of Jacob's trouble (Jer 30:7) so He can ". . . refine them like silver and test them like gold . . ." (Zech 13:9).

So, who are God's people during the church age? Paul is making it clear by quoting Hosea that it is NOT THE NATION OF ISRAEL! At the same time, the Bible is crystal clear that, at the end of the Tribulation, a remnant of Israel will again be GOD'S PEOPLE! That is one of the glorious themes of Zechariah!

Severe doctrinal problems can occur when one does not recognize the fact that Israel as a nation has been set aside in unbelief. For example, there is an erroneous doctrine gaining ground in some quarters known as "Dual-Covenant Theology".

Wikipedia defines Dual-Covenant Theology as: "Dual-covenant theology is a Liberal Christian view that holds that Jews may simply keep the Law of Moses, because of the 'everlasting covenant' (Genesis 17:13) between Abraham and God expressed in the Hebrew Bible, whereas Gentiles (those not Jews or Jewish proselytes) must convert to Christianity . . ."[13]

This teaching is in direct contradiction to Paul's inspired teaching in this regard. For example, we read in Romans 3:19-22:

Now we know that what things soever the law saith, it saith to them who are under the law: that every mouth may be stopped, and all the world may become guilty before God. Therefore by

---

13 https://en.wikipedia.org/wiki/Dual-covenant_theology

the deeds of the law there shall no flesh be justified in his sight: for by the law is the knowledge of sin. But now the righteousness of God without (apart from) the law is manifested, being witnessed by the law and the prophets; Even the righteousness of God, which is by faith of Jesus Christ unto all and upon all them that believe: for there is no difference (between Jews & Gentiles).

The Word of God is very clear. There is only one way of salvation, for Jew and Gentile alike, and that is through faith in Jesus Christ alone for our salvation. Any other gospel is a false gospel and Paul made it very clear that ". . . If any *man* preach any other gospel unto you than that ye have received, let him be accursed" (Gal 1:9).

Israel's Future Spiritual State Pre-Second Coming

In my view, the most significant prophetic fulfillment of the 20th century was the establishment of the Jewish state in 1948. After almost 1900 years of dispersion, in fulfillment of numerous Old and New Testament prophecies (cf. Hos 3:4, 5; 5:15-6:2; Ezek 37:12-14; Rom 11:25, 26), God has regathered His ancient people from the four corners of the earth back to their everlasting possession based on an everlasting covenant. When God established His covenant with Abraham, He promised in Genesis 17:7, 8:

And I will establish my covenant between me and thee and thy seed after thee in their generations for an *everlasting* covenant, to be a God unto thee, and to thy seed after thee. And I will give unto thee, and to thy seed after thee, the land wherein thou art a stranger, all the land of Canaan, for an *everlasting* possession; and I will be their God (italics added).

The Hebrew (*'olam*) is the word often translated by the English word *everlasting* and occurs twice in the above passage and a total of 439 times in the Hebrew Old Testament.[14] It is probably derived from *'alam*, "to hide," thus pointing to what is hidden in the distant future or in the distant past.[15] Most scholars agree that "the basic meaning . . . is farthest time, distant time."[16]

Having established that the return of Israel to the land is based on an *everlasting* covenant pertaining to an *everlasting* possession, let's proceed to give a brief history of Israel's conflicts pertaining to their possession of the land, and what the Scriptures predict regarding their future.

On May 14, 1948, the state of Israel was declared, followed the next morning by the first Arab-Israeli war. This invasion of the Jewish State involved the regular armies of Egypt, Transjordan, Iraq, Syria, and Lebanon, and contingents from Saudi Arabia.[17] This was followed in 1956 by a brief war with Egypt in the Gaza Strip and the Sinai Peninsula. The Six-Day War (1967) took place with Egypt, Jordan, Iraq and Syria, resulting in the reunification of Jerusalem under Israeli control. The Yom Kippur War (1973) took place when Egypt and Syria launched a coordinated attack on the Suez and Golan Heights. This, too, eventuated in an Israel victory.

The Bible indicates that there will be at least two future Arab/Israeli wars prior to the climactic worldwide assault against Jerusalem

14 Based upon the biblical computer search program of the NASB Accordance 11.2.1 for Mcintosh computers from Oak Tree Software, Inc.

15 R. Laird Harris, Gleason L. Archer Jr., Bruce K. Waltke, editors, 2 Vols., *Theological Wordbook of the Old Testament* (Chicago, IL: Moody Press, 1980), Vol. II, p. 672.

16 Willem A. VanGemeren, editor, *New International Dictionary of Old Testament Theology & Exegesis*, 5 Vols. (Grand Rapids, MI: Zondervan, 1997), Vol. 3, p. 346.

17 Hanan Sher, editor, *Facts About Israel*, (Jerusalem: Keter Press Enterprises, 1977), 53.

just prior to the second coming (Zech 14:2). These wars are "the inner circle" war (Israel's immediate neighbors) of Psalm 83, and "the outer ring" war (Israel's distant neighbors) of Ezekiel 38.[18]

I note these future wars in relation to Israel's future spiritual state prior to the second coming of Christ. In other words, what does the Bible say in regard to Israel's spiritual condition following their return to nationhood, but prior to the Lord's return to establish His millennial kingdom? To answer that, let me quote from Ezekiel 37:21-23, which is in the context of the future "outer ring" war commonly known as the battle of Gog and Magog:

> And say unto them, Thus saith the Lord God; Behold, I will take the children of Israel from among the heathen, whither they be gone and will gather them on every side, and bring them into their own land: And I will make them one nation in the land upon the mountains of Israel; and one king shall be king to them all: and they shall be no more two nations, neither shall they be divided into two kingdoms any more at all: Neither shall they defile themselves any more with their idols, nor with their detestable things, or with any of their transgressions: but I will save them out of all their dwellingplaces, wherein they have sinned, and will cleanse them: so shall they be my people and I will be their God.

God characterizes Israel at this future time as being "idolatrous," full of "detestable things" and "transgressions." What will Israel's reputation be among the nations during this future time? We read in Ezekiel 39:7:

---

18 Both of these wars are dealt with extensively by Bill Salus, *Psalm 83 The Missing Prophecy Revealed*, (La Quinta, CA: Prophecy Depot Ministries, 2013).

So will I make my holy name known in the midst of my people Israel; and I will not let them pollute my holy name any more: and the heathen shall know that I am the LORD, the Holy One in Israel.

The prophetic Scriptures declare that, at the time of this future war of Gog and Magog, Israel's reputation will be so bad that they are known as a nation that "pollutes" or "profanes" God's holy name.

How does all of this relate to the Christian's attitude toward the nation of Israel and the Jewish people residing therein? I believe we should rejoice in the fulfillment of Bible prophecy, in the miracle of Israel's restoration to the land. At the same time, we should recognize that they have been restored in a condition of unbelief and spiritual blindness (Rom 11:25). It is my view, therefore, that Christians are not obligated to endorse either the Jewish religion or carte blanche, every action of the Israeli government, while they are in a state of rebellion against God.

What we are obligated to do as Christians is, first of all, to be burdened for the salvation of the Jews. Paul stated in Romans 10:2-4a, ". . . I have great heaviness and continual sorrow in my heart. For I wish that myself were accursed from Christ for my brethren, my kinsmen according to the flesh: Who are Israelites . . ." This heaviness and sorrow led Paul to resolve: "Brethren, my heart's desire and prayer to God for Israel is, that they might be saved (Rom 10:1).

As Christians during these waning days of the Church Age, we need to be burdened to pray for the salvation of the Jews, and to take every opportunity to witness to them as well as support missionaries that are attempting to reach Jews for Jesus!

God's People in the Church Age

If the Jews are not God's people during the church age, then who is? Let's begin to answer that question by looking at Acts 15:14. During the Jerusalem Council of A.D. 48, the council moderator James declared: "Simeon (Peter) hath declared how God at the first did visit the Gentiles, to take out of them a people for his name." The Jerusalem Council was convened to deal with the issue of Gentiles being saved, and how they fit into the church.

In sorting out this issue James declared that God's purpose during the church age is visiting the Gentiles (*ethnos* – nations) to take out of them a people for His name. In other words, rather than focusing primarily on the Jews, God is now expanding His redemptive program to all the nations. This is something new, as Jesus Himself said, "I am not sent but unto the lost sheep of the house of Israel" (Matt 15:24). If the Jews are "not my people" during the church age, then who is? Paul answers that in Galatians 3:26-28:

> For ye are all the children of God by faith in Christ Jesus. For as many of you as have been baptized into Christ have put on Christ. There is neither Jew nor Greek, there is neither bond nor free, there is neither male nor female; for ye are all one in Christ Jesus.

So, who are the children of God in the church age? Not unbelieving Jews or the nation of Israel. Rather, according to the Word of God, the children of God in the church age consists of Jews and Gentiles ALIKE who have exercised faith in Jesus Christ. Paul further describes the spiritual equality of the children of God in the church age in Ephesians 2:13-16:

But in in Christ Jesus ye who sometimes were far off (Gentiles) are made nigh by the blood of Christ. For he is our peace, who hath made both one, and hath broken down the middle wall of partition between us; Having abolished in his flesh the enmity, even the law of commandments contained in ordinances; for to make in himself of twain one new man, so making peace. And that he might reconcile both (Jew and Gentile) unto God in one body by the cross, having slain the enmity thereby:

Paul refers to this as a "mystery," a surprise, something that was not previously revealed. Paul states in Ephesians 3:2-6:

If ye have heard of the dispensation of the grace of God which is given me to you-ward: How that by revelation he made known unto me the mystery . . . Which in other ages was not made known unto the sons of men, as it is now revealed unto his holy apostles and prophets by the Spirit; That the Gentiles should be fellow heirs, and of the same body, and partakers of his promise in Christ by the gospel:

CONCLUSION

In sum, Israel during the church age has been set aside in unbelief, until the conclusion of the "times of the gentiles" at the second coming. While some individual Jews are being saved during the church age, the preponderance of God's redemptive activity consists of calling out Gentiles from around the world to be a "people for His name" (Acts 15:14). While we should certainly pray for and work for the salvation of Jews as did the Apostle Paul (Rom 10:1), our Great Commission is to "Go therefore, and teach all nations . . ." (Matt 28:19).

If you are concerned about Jews coming to Christ, you should take Paul's advice and witness to Gentiles: "Have they (the Jews) stumbled that they should fall? God forbid: but rather through their fall salvation is come unto the Gentiles, for to provoke them (the Jews) to jealousy" (Rom 11:11). So if you want to see Jews get saved, witness to Gentiles, so the Jews will get jealous!

In our next chapter, we will chart how God is fulfilling Bible prophecy in these last days by regathering Jews from around the world back to the nation of Israel in preparation for the resumption of God's redemptive work with Israel in the Tribulation.

CHAPTER 3

The Regathering of Ethnic Israel

§

WE SAW IN OUR PREVIOUS chapter that the nation Israel has been set aside in unbelief during the present church age. However, as the church age draws to a close, God will begin to regather ethnic Israel from the four corners of the world in preparation for the Tribulation, the time of "Jacob's trouble" (Jer 30:7). This chapter will deal with the fulfillment of those promises.

THE PROPHESIED DISPERSION

Let's begin with prophecies pertaining to the dispersion of Israel as a result of their disobedience. Deuteronomy 28–32 deals with the "blessings" and "cursings" that would come to Israel based on their obedience or disobedience. One of the promised curses to disobedient Israel has to do with prophecies regarding their dispersion. Deuteronomy 28:63-66 states:

> And it shall come to pass that as the LORD rejoiced over you to do you good, and to multiply you; so the LORD will rejoice over you to destroy you, and to bring you to nought; and ye shall be plucked from off the land whither thou goest to possess it. And the LORD shall scatter thee among all people from

the one end of the Earth even unto the other; and there thou shall serve other gods, which neither thou nor thy fathers have known, *even* wood and stone. And among these nations shalt thou find no ease, neither shall the sole of thy foot have rest: but the Lord shall give thee there a trembling heart, and failing of eyes, and sorrow of mind: And thy life shall hang in doubt before thee; and thou shalt fear day and night, and shall have none assurance of thy life:

Since their dispersion in AD 70, the Bible predicted that the people of Israel would be subject to severe persecution in many nations. This prophecy has been literally fulfilled again and again even into modern times during the Nazi holocaust. According to this prophecy, there is apparently more persecution yet to come in the last days, even until the end of the Tribulation. We read in Zechariah 14:2: "And I will gather all nations against Jerusalem to battle: and the city shall be taken, and the houses rifled, and the women ravished: and half of the city shall go forth into captivity, and the residue of the people shall not be cut off from the city." This prophecy will find fulfillment just before the second coming of the Messiah, as we read in Zechariah 14:3, 4:

Then shall the LORD go forth, and fight against those nations, as when he fought in the day of battle. And his feet shall stand in that day upon the mount of Olives, which is before Jerusalem on the east, and the mount of Olives shall cleave in the midst thereof toward the east and toward the west, and there shall be a very great valley; and half of the mountain shall remove toward the north, and half of it toward the south.

The Prophesied Regathering

Just as the Bible predicted that Israel will be dispersed among the nations, so also does it predict their eventual regathering. We read in Hosea 3:4, 5:

> For the children of Israel shall abide many days without a king and without a prince and without a sacrifice, and without an image and without an ephod and without teraphim. Afterward shall the children of Israel return and seek the LORD their God, and David their king, and shall fear the LORD and his goodness in the latter days.

Hosea is here predicting a regathering of Israel after "many days." This will be a time when the children of Israel will return to seek the Lord "in the latter days." In Hosea 5:15-6:2 we may receive some clues as to the *timing* of this regathering:

> I will go *and* return to my place, till they acknowledge their offence, and seek my face: in their affliction they will seek me early. Come, and let us return unto the LORD: for he hath torn, and he will heal us; he hath smitten, and he will bind us up. After two days will he revive us: in the third day he will raise us up, and we shall live in his sight.

Two prophetic mysteries are suggested here. Jesus Christ, representing the true Israel in His death, was raised on the third day. Could it be that, likewise, the nation of Israel, seemingly "dead" for two thousand years, will be raised for her thousand-year millennial reign, when she returns to Messiah and He to her at the end of this present age? Keep in mind Peter's statement in 2 Peter 3:8 that, "one day is with the Lord as a thousand years." If that is so, and since Christ ascended to heaven in A.D. 29, could we be fast approaching that time when a remnant of Israel will be "raised again" to spiritual life through faith in Christ?

I believe this promised regathering, in preparation for Israel's repentance and revival, also accords well with what Ezekiel promises in 37:12-14:

> Therefore prophesy and say unto them, Thus saith the Lord God; Behold, O my people, I will open your graves, and cause you to come up out of your graves, and bring you into the land of Israel. And ye shall know that I am the LORD, when I have opened your graves, O my people, and brought you up out of your graves, And shall put my spirit in you, and ye shall live, and I shall place you in your own land: then shall ye know that I the LORD hath spoken *it*, and performed *it*, saith the LORD.

The Prophetic Order of the Regathering

Not only does the Bible predict that Israel will be regathered to her ancient homeland in the "latter days," but it also predicts the *order* of this regathering, in both the Old and New Testaments. In Isaiah 43 the prophet seeks to bring comfort to Israel by predicting her regathering in the latter days. Consider Isaiah 43:3-6:

> For I am the LORD thy God, the Holy One of Israel, thy Saviour: I gave Egypt for thy ransom, Ethiopia, and Seba for thee, Since thou wast precious in my sight, thou hast been honourable, and I have loved thee: therefore will I give men for thee, and people for thy life. Fear not, for I am with thee, I will bring thy seed from the east, and gather thee from the west; I will say to the north, Give up: and to the south, Keep not back:

bring my sons from far, and my daughters from the end of the earth.

The promised regathering, including the specific order of these events, is repeated in the New Testament. We read in Luke 13:29 where Jesus said, in reference to the kingdom of God during His millennial reign: "And they (Israel) shall come from the east, and from the west, and from the north, and from the south, and shall sit down in the kingdom of God." Let's consider how this prophetic order has been fulfilled exactly as promised in these latter days of the church age.

East (Middle East): I believe the regathering from the east refers to the Middle East. Beginning around 1900, Jews from Turkey, Jordan, Syria, Iraq, Yemen and other Middle Eastern nations began migrating to what was then known as Palestine. Almost 90% of Jews from these countries have migrated to Israel as of the present, and the migration continues.

West (Europe): In 1939, the Jewish population of Europe was 9,408,000. In 1948, it had dropped to 3,708,000. After the Nazi holocaust, in which almost six million Jews were killed, additional hundreds of thousands fled to Israel seeking a place of peace and safety. Because of rising anti-Semitism in Europe, we are seeing, once again, an acceleration of Jews returning to Israel from Europe.

North (Russia): Beginning in 1988, under the *glasnost* (openness) policies of Gorbachev, Jews were allowed to immigrate back to Israel. My longtime friend and mentor, Noah Hutchings, tells an interesting story in this regard:

The third phase of Jewish immigration, according to prophecy, was to come from the north. Until the *glasnost* policies of Gorbachev were initiated in Russia in 1988, the Jews were not allowed to emigrate. Then, a few began to return though Helsinki; but the prime minister of Finland closed the exit door because of Arab pressure. A constituent of our ministry, Siiki, and a friend of the prime minister's wife, informed him that unless he opened the door to Jewish emigration from Russia again, God would do to him what He did to the king of Edom. To date, over four hundred thousand Russian Jews have gone to Israel.[19]

South (Ethiopia): In 1991, under *Operation Solomon*, approximately 14,000 black Ethiopian Jews (known as Falasha) were flown to Israel, in a period of 72 hours. It is a fascinating story. But before I go into the details, we must go back in history.

According to tradition, the black Jews of Ethiopia were descendants of a son born to the Queen of Sheba by Solomon (1 Kings 10). One of the descendants of this union was purportedly the Ethiopian eunuch that Phillip led to the Lord in Acts 8:26-40. Through the next two millennia, Ethiopian Jews continued to multiply. In 1991, the ruler of Ethiopia decided he no longer wanted these Falasha Jews in his country. He contacted the President of Israel and gave him 72 hours to remove these Jews or they would be killed.

Israel immediately dispatched jumbo jets to Ethiopia, and in a period of 72 hours, transported approximately 14,000 of them to Israel, where they live today. Thus, the order of the return of a Jewish remnant to await Messiah's appearance is exactly as prophesied. This immigration from the four corners of the globe continues today. This is one of the most amazing fulfillments of Bible prophecy in the church age.

---

19 Noah W. Hutchings, *40 Irrefutable Signs of the Last Generation* (Oklahoma City: Bible Belt Publishing, 2010) 131.

Because of this miraculous regathering, in fulfillment of ancient prophecies, there are now ethnic Jews that have returned to Israel from every nation in the world. The latest population figures indicate a current population in Israel of 7.4 million – 6 million Jews and approximately 1.4 million Arabs. Even though most Jews have returned from many countries because of persecution, in due course it will be revealed to them the real reason, which is for them to say, "Blessed is He who comes in the name of the Lord" when Jesus returns to save a remnant of Israel at His second coming.

What we have seen since around the year 1900 is God, providentially, and in fulfillment of His ancient promises, regathering ethnic Jews from around the world in preparation for the resumption of God's focus on His chosen nation. Though the nation Israel is presently set aside in unbelief, as we saw in Hosea and Romans, God is regathering the nation in preparation for the resumption of His national plan. This preparation will intensify during Daniel's 70th week (Dan 9:24-27), the Tribulation Period.

Jeremiah speaks of this in Jeremiah 30:7-11:

> Alas! For that day is great, so that none is like it: it is even the time of Jacob's trouble; but he shall be saved out of it. For it shall come to pass in that day, saith the LORD of hosts, that I will break his yoke from off thy neck, and will burst thy bonds, and strangers shall no more serve themselves of him: But they shall serve the LORD their God, and David their king, whom I will raise up unto them. Therefore fear thou not, O my servant Jacob, saith the LORD; neither be dismayed, O Israel: for, lo, I will save thee from afar, and thy seed from the land of their captivity; and Jacob shall return, and shall be in rest, and be quiet, and none shall make him afraid. For I am with thee, saith

the LORD, to save thee: though I make a full end of all nations whither I have scattered thee, yet will I not make a full end of thee: but I will correct thee in measure, and will not leave thee altogether unpunished.

Up until this point in the book of Jeremiah, the prophet dealt with near term events pertaining to Judah's Babylonian exile (606-536 BC) and their post-exilic return. In this second division of Jeremiah (chapters 30-36) we see a transition to prophecies that will be fulfilled far beyond the events of the immediate exile and return. Jeremiah predicts an even greater exile and period of trouble awaiting Israel. Despite the scattering, persecution and trouble, culminating in the Tribulation, Jeremiah predicts that Israel will finally be saved and be at rest. Thus the curse of dispersion and trouble, first predicted in Deuteronomy, will finally be over, and Israel will once again find favor from God and rest among the nations.

What we are seeing today, in the regathering of unbelieving Israel from the four corners of the earth, is in preparation for that glorious day of national repentance and restoration. That is but one of many themes we will be exploring in the book of Zechariah.

CHAPTER 4

Overview of Zechariah

§

THE PRIMARY PURPOSE OF THIS book is to focus on the Messianic prophecies pertaining to the first and second advents of Jesus Christ and the future of Israel in the near and long term. However, a secondary purpose is to acquaint the reader with introductory issues (chapter one) and the overall structure and content of the book. This is what will be covered in this chapter.

STRUCTURE OF ZECHARIAH

Zechariah may be divided into two major parts, as found in chapters 1-8 and 9-14. Within those two major sections, it likewise falls rather naturally into five major divisions, as seen below:

PART I (CHAPTERS 1-8)

    I. The Introduction to the Book (1:1-6)
        A. The Date and the Author's Name (1:1)
        B. A Call to Repentance (1:2-6)
    II. A Series of Eight Night Visions (1:7-6:8)
        A. The First Vision: The Horseman Among the Myrtle Trees (1:7-17)

PART II (CHAPTERS 9-14)

The second main section of the book deals with two prophetic oracles. These deal primarily with Messianic prophecies concerning Israel's future and the full realization of the Theocracy.

4. Warning and encouragement (10:2-4)
5. Israel's victory over her enemies (10:5-7)
6. Israel's complete deliverance and restoration (10:8-12)
B. The rejection of the Messianic Shepherd-King (11:1-17)
1. The prologue (11:1-3)
2. The prophecy of the rejection of the Good Shepherd (11:4-14)
3. The worthless shepherd (11:15-17)
II. The Second Oracle: The Advent and Reception of the Messiah (12:1-14:21)
A. The deliverance and conversion of Israel (12:1-13:9)
1. The siege of Jerusalem (12:1-3)
2. The divine deliverance (12:4-9)
3. Israel's complete deliverance from sin (12:10-13:9)
4. The Messiah's return and his kingdom (14:1-21)
a. The siege of Jerusalem (14:1, 2)
b. The token of the Messiah's return (14:3-8)
c. The establishment of Messiah's kingdom (14:9-11)
d. The punishment of Israel's enemies (14:12-15)
e. The universal worship of the King (14:16-19)
f. "HOLY TO THE LORD" (14:20, 21)

Overview of Chapters 1-8

The date and authorship of the book is given in 1:1: "In the eighth month, in the second year of Darius, came the word of the Lord unto Zechariah, the son of Berechiah, the son of Iddo the prophet . . ."

The eighth month of Darius's second year was, by our calendar's reckoning, October-November 520 B.C. At the time of Israel's return from the Babylonian exile, she had no king of her own to date events by. So Zechariah's prophecy had to be dated by the reign of Darius, king of

Persia and Suzerain of Judah. The "word of the Lord" is a technical term for the prophetic word of revelation. When reference is made to the coming of the word of the Lord, the historical character of the word of God is referred to. But elsewhere God's word not only "comes," it also "comes true," or is fulfilled. We will see both aspects in the book of Zechariah.

This "word of the Lord' initially is a call to repentance, as seen in 1:2-6. The heart of the exhortation is seen in verse 3: "turn ye unto me, saith the Lord of hosts and I will turn unto you . . ." Zechariah is making a plea for a wholehearted response to the Lord's invitation to return to Him. If they will do so, the covenant relationship will be renewed and spiritual restoration will accompany the material restoration of the post-exilic temple.

The call to repent is followed by a series of eight night visions (1:7-6:8). In a series of eight apocalyptic visions on a single night, God revealed His purpose for the future of Israel—Jerusalem and Judah in particular, since Jerusalem was the seat of the Davidic dynasty and the place of the Lord's throne in the temple. Each vision contributes to the total picture of the role of Israel in the new post-exilic era about to dawn and was intended as an encouragement to the people in the work of rebuilding the temple as well as to promote the spiritual renewal of the people of Judah.

These eight visions are followed by the symbolic crowning of Joshua as the high priest (6:9-15). The position of this actual ceremony after the eight visions is significant. The fourth and fifth visions were concerned with the high priest and the civil governor in the Davidic line. Zechariah here linked the message of those two visions to the Messianic King-Priest. We read of this Messianic King-Priest in 6:12, 13:

Behold the man whose name is the BRANCH; and he shall grow up out of his place, and he shall build the temple of the

LORD: Even he shall build the temple of the LORD; and he shall bear the glory, and shall sit and rule upon his throne; and he shall be a priest upon his throne: and the counsel of peace shall be between them both.

In the fourth vision (ch. 3), Joshua was priest. In Zechariah 6:13, the Branch was to officiate as priest. In the fifth vision (ch. 4), Zerubbabel was the governing civil official. In Zechariah 6:13 the Branch was to rule the government. In 4:9, Zerubbabel was to complete the rebuilding of the temple. In 6:12, the Branch would build the millennial temple. In 4:14 Zerubbabel and Joshua represent two separate offices; here the Branch was to hold both offices (6:13). Thus restored Israel is seen in the future under the glorious reign of the Messianic King-Priest.

In the book of Zechariah, Joshua served as a type of the Messiah, but at certain points the language transcends the experience of the type and becomes more directly prophetical of the antitype, the Messiah. The crowning of King-Priest Messiah is thus set forth symbolically by the coronation of Joshua, which evidently took place the day following the night of visions (6:9-15).

The next section (7:1-8:23) deals with the problem of fasting and the promises of the future. This section begins with an inquiry from the people of Bethel as to whether they should continue to observe a national fast, which had been instituted during the Babylonian captivity (7:3). Zechariah's answer falls into four sections, each of which is introduced by the same formula "the word of the LORD came unto Zechariah. . ." (7:4, 8; 8:1, 18). The purpose of chapters seven and eight is to impress upon the people their need to live righteously in response to their past judgment and future glory.

Overview of Chapters 9-14

Having given a quick overview of chapters one through eight, we now move to part two of the book, chapters nine through fourteen. In this section, we deal with the prophetic oracles that pertain to Israel's great Messianic future and the full realization of the theocracy. While chapter one through eight contains occasional glimpses of future events, chapters nine through fourteen are almost exclusively eschatological (future events). The future orientation is rendered more certain by the 18 occurrences of the phrase "on that day." The theme of part two (chapters 9-14) centers on the judgments and blessings that accompany the appearance of the Messianic King. There are two oracles in this section of the book.

The First Oracle

The first oracle deals with the advent and rejection of the Messiah (9:1-11:7). In this section, there are many amazing prophecies concerning the first advent of Christ. We will deal with these in survey form here, and consider them in greater detail in subsequent chapters of this book.

The advent of the Messianic King is dealt with in 9:1-10:12. In 9:1-8 we learn about the destruction of nations and preservation of Zion. The mood of the first oracle is characterized by *change*. In the midst of judgment (9:1-7), Israel finds deliverance (9:8). Thus 9:1-8 is a prophetic description of the Lord's march south to Jerusalem, destroying the traditional enemies of Israel, such as Syria, Tyre, Sidon and Ashdod. The agent of this destruction is Alexander the Great, as he advanced on his warhorse south from Aram (Syria), subjugating city after city.

The advent of Zion's King is celebrated in 9:9, 10. The jubilation is not over Alexander the Great but over a new Sovereign, who will come, not on a warhorse, but on a donkey. The prophet describes His character as just and, therefore, saving; He is lowly and, therefore, peaceful. In contrast to Alexander's empire, which was founded on bloodshed, the Messianic King will establish a universal kingdom of peace.

This is followed by the deliverance and blessing of Zion's people (9:11-10:1). Although the Messiah's mission is to establish His kingdom of "peace," He must first conquer all enemies and deliver His people. This He sets out to do (9:11-16). Before He can reign in peace, He must fully deliver and restore Israel. This passage is filled with battle terminology: prisoners (v. 11), fortress (v. 12), bow (v. 13), sword (v. 13), arrow (v. 14), trumpet (v. 14), and sling stones (v 15). With Israel's deliverance at Christ's second coming comes blessing, including agricultural prosperity and favorable weather.

The next section (10:2-4) provides Israel with warning and encouragement. Zechariah warned Israel's idolatrous leaders (vv 2-3a), but encouraged the people (vv 3b-4). Prayer to God brings blessing (v. 1), but trust in idols produces disappointment and sorrow (v. 2). In the next section (10:5-7), Israel's victory over her enemies is predicted. The Lord promises to make Israel mighty and to reunite and restore the nation, causing the people to rejoice in Him. In this prophetic passage, God's people win against superior odds. Although the final, complete fulfillment doubtless will be at Christ's second coming perhaps the first stage in the progressive fulfillment of the passage is to be found in the Maccabean victories (second century, B.C.).

The following section (10:8-12) predicts Israel's complete deliverance and restoration. The Lord promises to regather His people from distant lands. He will strengthen them and the power of their ancient oppressors, such as Egypt and Assyria, will wane. As a result of the Lord's regathering and strengthening Israel, the will ". . . walk up and down in his name . . ." (10:12).

The next section (11:1-17) deals with the rejection of the Messianic Shepherd-King. A calamity to befall Israel is described in verses 1-3 and the cause of that calamity is dealt with in verses 4-14. The cause of the calamity is the people's rejection of the Messianic Shepherd-King (11:4-14) at His first advent. Judas' betrayal of Jesus is graphically predicted in verses 12-13, resulting in the rejection of Israel (v 14): "Then I cut asunder mine other staff, even Bands, that I might break the brotherhood between Judah and Israel."

This verse signifies the destruction or dissolution of the covenant nation, particularly of the unity between the south and the north. The catastrophic rejection by Israel of their Messiah resulted in the subsequent breakup of the Jewish commonwealth at the hands of the Romans in A.D. 70. Yet, even this new destruction and dispersion are not permanent; otherwise there would be no point in promises pertaining to Israel's future deliverance, regathering, and restoration in the succeeding chapters.

The message of the first oracle concludes with a description of the worthless shepherd (11:15-17). With the Shepherd of the Lord's choice removed from the scene, a foolish and worthless shepherd replaces Him. The worthless shepherd is here characterized as "foolish," a word denoting one who is morally deficient. Instead of feeding the sheep, he will feed on them—preying on the unwary. Although the identity of this worthless shepherd is not revealed, it seems that the final stage of this prophecy awaits the rise of the final Antichrist (Daniel 11:36-39; Revelation 13:1-8).

The curse calls for his power ("arm") to be paralyzed ("completely withered") and his intelligence ("right eye") to be frustrated or nullified ("totally blinded"). For the fulfillment with respect to the Antichrist or "beast," see Revelation 19:19-21; 20:10. The judgment here (11:17) brings to a close the cycle of prophecy which began with judgment (9:1). Thus, the first oracle of part two ends on a note of sadness.

THE SECOND ORACLE

The Second Oracle deals with the advent and reception of the Messiah (12:1-14:21). This oracle forms the joyous climax of the book. It includes the siege of Jerusalem (12:1-3) and the divine deliverance (12:4-9). This is followed by Israel's complete deliverance from sin (12:10-13:9). This section begins with a day of national repentance when the remnant of Israel recognizes the one ". . . whom they have pierced, and they shall mourn for him, as one mourneth for his only son . . ." (12:10).

This mourning and repentance results in a fountain of forgiveness and cleansing being opened for the nation Israel (13:1). This section culminates with the declaration: "And I will bring the third part through the fire, and will refine them as silver is refined, and will try them as gold is tried: they shall call on my name, and I will hear them: I will say, It is my people: and they shall say, The Lord is my God."

At the end of the Tribulation, at the second coming of Christ, a remnant of Israel, consisting of one third of their numbers, will repent of their murder of the Messiah and will receive forgiveness and cleansing. As a result, the curse of Hosea 1:9 is reversed, where God declares, ". . . Call his name Lo-ammi: for ye are not my people, and I will not be your God." After two millennia of dispersion and persecution because of unbelief, Israel, once again, becomes God's people. Thus Romans 11:25, 26 will be fulfilled: ". . . blindness in part is happened to Israel, until the fullness of the Gentiles be come in. And so all Israel shall be saved: as it is written, There shall come out of Sion the Deliverer, and shall turn away ungodliness from Jacob."

Chapter 14 deals with the Messiah's return and His kingdom. The chapter begins with the siege of Jerusalem as described in 14:1, 2:

> Behold the day of the LORD cometh, and thy spoil shall be divided in the midst of thee. For I will gather all nations against Jerusalem to battle; and the city shall be taken, and the houses rifled, and the women ravished; and half of the city shall go forth into captivity, and the residue of the people shall not be cut off from the city.

Jerusalem will once again be trodden down by the Gentiles, as all nations will fight against it, plundering, ransacking and raping, resulting in the capture of the city. This will only cease at Christ's second coming, as seen in verse three: "Then shall the LORD go forth, and fight against those nations, as when he fought in the day of battle." Since Zechariah 14:2 clearly indicates that Jerusalem will be "trampled on" by the Gentiles again in the future, it appears that the "times of the Gentiles" (Luke 21:24) will extend to the Messiah's second advent.

Jesus refers to this "trodding down" by the Gentiles in Luke 21:24: "And they [the Jews] shall fall by the edge of the sword, and shall be led away captive into all nations: and Jerusalem shall be trodden down of the Gentiles, until the times of the Gentiles be fulfilled." Henry Morris says, in regard to this verse:

> Jerusalem, the great capital city of the Jews, continued to be under Gentile control until the Israelis recaptured it from the Arabs in 1967. In fact, the essential area of Jerusalem—that is, the sacred site of its ancient temple—is still to this day under control of the Muslim Arabs. Thus, the "times of the Gentiles" have not yet been fulfilled, nor will they be until Christ returns to reign there.[20]

---

20 H. Morris, *The Henry Morris Study Bible.* Green Forest, AR, 2012), 1551.

The Messiah's return, according to 14:3-8, will include the following: He will land on the Mount of Olives (14:3) in fulfillment of Acts 1:11, 12. His landing will cause a great earthquake on the Mount of Olives. It will cause unique meteorological changes, resulting in a day without daytime or nighttime (14:7), and it will cause water to flow out from Jerusalem toward the Mediterranean Sea and the Dead Sea. Perhaps this unexplained event will be caused by the massive earthquake that is predicted for this region.

The establishment of the Messiah's kingdom follows (14:9-11) along with the punishment of Israel's enemies (14:12-15). This will be followed by the universal worship of Christ the King (14:16-19). In spite of the awful decimation predicted in verses 12-15, there will be survivors – a converted remnant from those nations - who will make an annual pilgrimage to Jerusalem to "worship the King" (14:16). This worship will include celebrating the festival of tabernacles, as this festival seems to speak of the final, joyful regathering of Israel in full kingdom blessings, as well as of the ingathering of the nations.

The prophet next unfolds what will happen to the recalcitrant nations that refused to send delegations to this annual pilgrimage (14:17-19). Interestingly, the withholding of rain to these nations is reminiscent of the curses for covenant disobedience contained in Deuteronomy 28:22-24.

The book of Zechariah concludes with a depiction of the Messianic kingdom (14:20, 21). It is characterized by a pervasive holiness that will be inscribed on the bells of the horses, and cooking pots in the home and sacred bowls in the Millennial Temple. In Christ's kingdom no one who is morally or spiritually unclean will have access to the house of the Almighty.

Having given an overview of this marvelous prophetic book, in the next chapter we will consider the night visions given to Zechariah in 1:7-3:10.

CHAPTER 5

Night Visions I: 1:7-3:10

§

THE INTRODUCTION TO THE BOOK of Zechariah (1:1-6) deals with issues that normally characterize the beginning of the inspired writing. These are issues such as the time of writing, which took place in "the second year of Darius" in 519 BC (v 1). Authorship is ascribed to "Zechariah, the son of Berechiah, the son of Iddo" (v 1). Zechariah means "Jehovah remembers" and he was the most prolific writer among the "Minor Prophets" as Zechariah is the longest book in the Minor Prophets. Zechariah was both a priest and a prophet, being the grandson of another prophet, Iddo. He is mentioned in Nehemiah as coming to Jerusalem with Zerubbabel during reconstruction efforts in the post-exilic period (Ne 11:14; 12:16). The theme of the book is a call to repentance as is seen in 1:3: "Therefore say thou unto them, Thus saith the LORD of hosts; Turn ye unto me, saith the LORD of hosts, and I will turn unto you . . ."

After these opening words, probably delivered to the assembled people of post-exilic Judah, the visions were not only given in one night, but just as one followed rapidly the other, so are they all closely connected and describing events which are to follow one after the other. This revelation may fitly be termed "the Apocalypse of Zechariah." These night visions will occupy the balance of this chapter and next.

Horse Among the Myrtle Trees 1:7-17

In this first vision, Zechariah sees a Man riding upon a red horse and He halts in a valley among myrtle trees. He is surrounded by a large army of angels upon red, sorrel and white horses, and the Man upon the red horse becomes the center of the hosts of heaven. In the first place, note that the color of the horse which He rode was red; this denotes blood, and is the color of the Son of God, the lamb slain from the foundation of the world.

The angels give their reports to the Man in the midst, who is also called the Angel of the Lord, who is probably the preincarnate Christ. The Angel of the Lord becomes the intercessor for Jerusalem and turns to Jehovah, sitting upon His throne. The angel speaks in 1:12, ". . . O LORD of hosts, how long wilt thou not have mercy on Jerusalem and on the cities of Judah, against which thou hast had indignation three threescore and ten years?" Jehovah responds with comforting words:

> I am jealous for Jerusalem and for Zion with a great jealousy. And I am very sore displeased with the heathen that are at ease . . . I am returned to Jerusalem with mercies: my house shall be built in it, saith the LORD of hosts, and a line shall be stretched forth upon Jerusalem . . . My cities through prosperity shall yet be spread abroad; and the LORD shall yet comfort Zion, and shall yet choose Jerusalem (1:14-17).

The 70 years of prophesied exile in Babylon had passed and a remnant of Jews had returned to Judah. Yet they had still not rebuilt the temple, which they had been commissioned to do. These visions given to Zechariah are intended to encourage and constrain them to complete it.

Could this prophecy not also portend a more long-term fulfillment? The nations are at ease, prosperous and increased, and Jerusalem trodden down, the land waste and desolate, in the hands of the enemy. Is this not predictive of the great dispersion of Israel until their latter day regathering, which will eventually lead to repentance and regeneration?

FOUR HORNS AND FOUR CARPENTERS 1:18-21

The second night vision of Zechariah is closely connected with the first. In the first vision the time is given when the Lord will turn in mercy to Jerusalem – the time with the nations are at ease, and having helped forward the affliction of His people, are ripe for judgment. The scenes have passed away, and now the prophet lifts his eyes again and he sees *four horns*. We read this second vision in 1:18-21:

> Then lifted I up mine eyes, and saw, and behold four horns. And I said unto the angel that talked with me, What be these? And he answered me, These are the horses which have scattered Judah, Israel, and Jerusalem. And the LORD shewed me four carpenters. Then said I, What come these to do? And he spake, saying, These are the horns which have scattered Judah, so that no man did lift up his head: but these are come to fray them, to cast out the horns of the Gentiles, which lifted up their horn over the land of Judah to scatter it.

Let's identify the symbols that are used in this vision. First we have "four horns." The "horn," when used symbolically in Scripture, is a symbol of power and pride, and in prophecy stands for a kingdom and for political power. For example, we read in Revelation 17:12: "And the ten horns which thou sawest are ten kings, which have received no kingdom as yet; but receive power as kings one hour with the beast." In Zechariah 1:18-21, the "four horns" probably refer to the four great kingdoms of Daniel 2:32-44 that comprise the "times of the Gentiles."

You will recall from Nebuchadnezzar's image that those king-doms are the Babylonian, Medo-Persian, the Grecian and the Roman empires. The latter is still in existence through the European Union and will be a world power until the stone smites the image at its feet and pulverizes it. These horns are not identified by their nationality but by their function in this night vision. Their function is revealed in verse 20: ". . . These are the horns which have scattered Judah, Israel, and Jerusalem." Jewish history reveals that each of these empires did just that, culminating in the Roman dispersion of the Jews in A.D. 70.

The next symbol in this vision is "four carpenters." Their purpose is revealed in 1:21: ". . . These are come to fray them, to cast out the horns of the Gentiles, which lifted up their horn over the land of Judah to scatter it." The idea behind the word "fray" is the idea of destruc-tion or casting down. Zechariah is teaching that the four horns are overcome by four carpenters whose role is to cast down the horns of the nation. It does not necessarily follow that the four carpenters must be four other powers. The vision seems to teach two facts: first, the horns will be broken and cast down; and in the second place, God has for every hostile power which has sinned and sins against His people a corresponding greater power to overcome it, break into pieces and cast it down. Indeed, historically each of these "horns" has been cast down – Babylon by Medo-Persia (538 B.C.), Persia by Greece (334 B.C.), Greece by Rome (129 B.C.) and Rome in its final extension, as the religious Babylon of Revelation 18, ultimately cast down by Christ Himself.

There is also a possible final fulfillment during the time of "Jacob's trouble" (Jer 30:7). The elements of all four world powers will per-haps convene in the onslaught on Jerusalem – a confederacy of nations, indeed representatives from all nations, will come against Jerusalem during the Great Tribulation. We read of this in Zechariah 14:2, 3:

For I will gather all nations against Jerusalem to battle; and the city shall be taken, and the houses rifled, and the women ravished; and half of the city shall go forth into captivity, and the residue of the people shall not be cut off from the city. Then shall the LORD go forth, and fight against those nations, as when he fought in the day of battle.

In this passage we see that elements of all the four world powers will then in some way be convened in the onslaught on Jerusalem – a confederacy involving representatives of all nations will come up against Jerusalem, and it will be then that the four horns are broken by the four smiths and the casting down will be done.

MAN AND MEASURING LINE 2:1-13

The third night vision is one of the most interesting and instructive. As the third one, it forms the climax of the "good and comfortable" words which were spoken concerning Jerusalem. The number three stands in the Word of God for resurrection, life from the dead. For example, in Hosea, we read concerning Israel, "After two days will he revive us: in the third day he will raise us up, and we will live in his sight" (Ho 6:2).

In this third vision Zechariah sees the glorious restoration of Israel, which has been the burden of so many prophecies, and the glory which is connected with that restoration. In this night vision Zechariah hears of a restoration and of a glory which has never yet been fulfilled in the history of God's people. While some posit that this prophecy has already been fulfilled, the clue that this vision has yet to be fulfilled is that it will take place after the enemies of Israel have been cast down (Zech 1:21). Let's read of that restoration in Zechariah 2:10-12:

Sing and rejoice, O daughter of Zion: for, lo, I come, and I will dwell in the midst of thee, saith the LORD. And many nations shall be joined to the LORD in that day, and shall be my people: and I will dwell in the midst of thee, and thou shalt know that the LORD of hosts hath sent me unto thee. And the LORD shall inherit Judah his portion in the holy land, and shall choose Jerusalem again.

There can be no doubt that we are privileged to see the beginning of this regathering of the Jewish nation to the land of the fathers in unbelief, as we examined in chapter three. This regathering is preparatory for the future spiritual restoration this third night vision portends.

We may divide the third night vision into two parts. In the first part a man is seen with a measuring line measuring Jerusalem, and the restoration of the city and its enlargement is promised; in the other part promises of blessing are given as well as glimpses of the glory which will attend the restoration. This measurement is of the earthly city of Jerusalem and is reminiscent of Ezekiel's measurement of the millennial temple (Ezek 41) as well as the measurement of the New Jerusalem in the eternal state (Rev 21:16).

It is obvious that the Jerusalem measured in this third vision is the Jerusalem of the Millennium as it is as ". . . towns without walls for the multitude of men and cattle therein . . ." (2:4) protected by ". . . a wall of fire round about, and will be the glory in the midst of her" (2:5). The influx of men and cattle to Jerusalem will be so enormous that the city must be enlarged and it will spread out into the plain, without the need for protective walls. Zechariah's vision shows what the condition of Jerusalem will be in the beginning of the Millennium. The reason for Jerusalem's peace, security and prosperity will be the glory of the

Lord. This glory will be in the midst of the city, and will also form a wall of fire about the city. Glory and defense are here combined.

We have now in this vision a continued description of that happy condition of Jerusalem and all that is connected with it. First, we notice the summons for the Jews who are then still in dispersion in 2:6-7: "Ho, ho, come forth, and flee from the land of the north, saith the LORD: for I have spread you abroad as the four winds of the heaven, saith the Lord. Deliver thyself, O Zion, that dwellest with the daughter of Babylon."

Is it not to be expected that when the glory appears and the King of Glory comes again and His feet stand on the Mount of Olives, that the entire Jewish nation will then live in the land? This will not be the case. At this early stage of the Millennium described here, the Lord summons those Jews still in dispersion to return to the land of promise.

CLEANSING OF THE HIGH PRIEST 3:1-10

The fourth vision is like the first and second, closely connected with the foregoing one. It gives the crowning event of Israel's restoration. The prophet recognized in the figure which is seen by him Joshua the high priest, who is standing before the angel of the Lord, while at his right hand stands Satan to oppose him. Joshua was not clothed with his clean, priestly robes, but he wears filthy garments. Jehovah rebukes Satan and refers to Jerusalem as a "brand plucked from the fire" (3:2). After the accuser is rebuked, the filthy garments of the high priest are removed, his iniquity is forgiven, and he is clothed with festal raiment.

The prophet is so carried away with the vision that he asks that a clean mitre be put upon his head. A mitre was the official headdress of the ancient Jewish high priest. And now, after the high priest is thus clothed, the angel of the Lord charges him with an important message:

"If thou wilt walk in my ways and if thou wilt keep my charge, then thou shalt also judge my house and shalt also keep my courts, and I will give thee places to walk among these that stand by" (Zech 3:7). The servant is promised, and the stone which is laid before Joshua, is to have seven eyes. The iniquity of this land is to be removed in one day, and the vision closes with the scene of every man living in peace with his neighbor, each under their own vine and fig tree.

The high priest Joshua stands here for Jerusalem and for the sinful nation of Israel. Disobedience and sin have been the cause of Israel's misfortune and Jerusalem's ruin. What would a restoration of Israel to the land be without a healing of their sins and a regeneration of the nation? It is this divine forgiveness and cleansing of the nation which is here so wonderfully depicted in this vision.

Conclusion

We have seen in these four night visions various apocalyptic pictures of the nation Israel. In the vision of the horses among the myrtle trees (1:7-17), we see the predicted dispersion of Israel until their latter day regathering. In the vision of the four horns and four carpenters (1:18-21), we see the prediction regarding the gentile empires which comprise Israel's enemies and their eventual destruction. In the vision of the man and the measuring line (2:1-13) we learn about the future blessedness of Jerusalem in the millennium. In the vision of the cleansing of the high priest (3:1-10) we see the crowning events of Israel's restoration. In the next chapter, we will continue to examine the eight night visions that were given to the prophet Zechariah.

CHAPTER 6

Night Visions II: 3:11-6:8

§

IN THE LAST CHAPTER, WE began a study of the eight night visions that were given to Zechariah. These are apocalyptic in nature and deal with the future of Israel. We covered four of those visions in the last chapter and will deal with the remaining four visions in this chapter.

THE CANDLESTICK AND OLIVE TREES (4:1-14)

The first three chapters of Zechariah are the foundation of the entire book. The events in these chapters are again and again touched upon in the following visions and prophecies of Zechariah. For this reason we have paid special attention to these chapters, which speak so clearly of the time of Israel's restoration, the restoration itself and the different events connected with it.

There was a rest for the prophet between the fourth and fifth night vision. He had fallen into a deep sleep. He may have been overcome by the grand and important visions, and is now awakened by the angel with the question in 4:2, "What seest thou?" The new vision is a very striking one. The vision consists of "a candlestick all of gold, with a bowl upon the top of it, and his seven lamps thereon, and seven pipes to the seven lamps, which upon the top thereof: And two olives trees by it, one upon the right side of the bowl and the other upon the left side thereof" (4:2-3). The question of the prophet then follows, "What are these, my lord?" (4:4) is answered by the angel with this statement, "This is the word of the LORD unto Zerubbabel, saying, Not by might, nor by power, but by my spirit, saith the LORD of hosts" (4:6). The prophet then proceeds with the interpretation of these symbols.

It must be acknowledged that the vision of the candlestick and the two olive trees is one of the most difficult in the Bible and needs prayerful and thoughtful study. First, it is to be noted that the vision is one which speaks of perfection, completion, and fullness. The perfect and divine number seven is found three times in the vision; seven lamps, seven pipes, and seven eyes. The seven lamps are united to one stem, and above it is a golden bowl. The great mountain becomes a plain. The top stone is brought forth and crowns the building which is finished by Zerubbabel.

Zerubabbel here is a type of the Prince of Peace, Israel's king. His hands have laid the foundation, just as Zerubbabel has laid the foundation of the temple. Even as Zerubabbel will finish the second temple, bringing forth the headstone, so will Christ lay the foundation of the millennial temple and will bring it to completion. When this happens, it will be greeted with shoutings, crying ". . . grace, grace . . ." (4:7).

This is followed by a promise that the post-exilic temple would be completed: "The hands of Zerubbabel have laid the foundation of this house; his hands shall also finish it; and thou shalt know that the Lord of hosts hath sent me unto you. For who hath despised the day of small things?" (Zech 4:9, 10a). Keep in mind that one of the primary purposes of the book of Zechariah is to encourage the Judeans to complete the rebuilding of the temple, which they eventually did in 516 B.C. The new temple was indeed small in relation to the former temple (Ezra 3:12), yet it was a necessary beginning and its ramifications would eventually encompass the whole world. This is a reminder that no work done in the name of Christ as led by His Spirit and in harmony with

His Word is trivial in the eyes of God, for He can use small things to accomplish great things.

Zechariah then queries, "What are these two olive trees upon the right side of the candlestick and upon the left side thereof?" (Zech 4:11). The angel replies, "These are the two anointed ones (lit. "sons of fresh oil"), that stand by the Lord of the whole earth" (Zech 4:14). It appears that there are at least two layers of interpretation. There can be no doubt that these "sons of oil," as they are called, represented Joshua and Zerubbabel, living at the time of Zechariah, the one the priest and the other the king.

These two olive trees are likewise seen in Revelation 11:3-4: "And I will give power unto my two witnesses, and they shall prophecy a thousand two hundred and threescore days clothed in sackcloth. These are the two olive trees, and the two candlesticks standing before the God of the earth." Here they are the two witnesses who give their testimony during the Tribulation in Jerusalem, and who stand in direct relation to that theocracy which is then about to be established in Israel. Some suggest that these two witnesses are Moses and Elijah, the same who appeared with our Lord upon the mountain of transfiguration. Others suggest that Enoch and Elijah are the two witnesses, as they are the only Old Testament saints who were translated prior to death. Time will tell.

THE VISION OF THE FLYING ROLL (5:1-4)

The first five night visions were visions of comfort for Jerusalem and Judah, the overthrow of Babylon and all Judah's enemies, divine forgiveness and the restoration of the theocracy. Now follow the last three visons, and these are visions of judgment. Judgment precedes Israel's restoration and is very prominently connected with it. Following is the fifth vision:

Then I turned, and lifted up mine eyes, and looked, and behold a flying roll. And he said unto me, What seest thou? And I answered, I see a flying roll; the length thereof is twenty cubits, and the breadth thereof ten cubits. Then said he unto me, This is the curse that goeth forth over the face of the whole earth: for every one that stealeth shall be cut off as on this side according to it; and every one that sweareth shall be cut off as on that side according to it. I will bring it forth, saith the LORD of hosts, and it shall enter into the house of the thief, and into the house or him that sweareth falsely by my name: and it shall remain in the midst of his house, and shall consume it with the timber thereof and the stones thereof (Zech 5:1-4).

The prophet's eyes seem to have been closed after the fifth vision, for we read, "And I turned, and lifted up mine eyes" (5:1). The flying roll he sees is twenty cubits long and ten cubits broad. A biblical cubit is approximately 18 inches long. Thus the flying roll is approximately 30 feet long and 15 feet wide, which is quite large. The interpreting angel tells the prophet that it is the curse that goes forth over the face of the whole earth (5:3). That this vision means judgment is evident at the first glance. Ezekiel had a similar vision in Ezekiel 2:9, 10:

And when I looked, behold, an hand was sent unto me; and, lo, a roll of a book was therein. And he spread it before me; and it was written within and without: and there was written therein lamentations and mourning and woe.

The flying roll of Zechariah five is written on both sides, signifying the two tablets of stone, the law of God. Stealing and swearing falsely are mentioned because the one is found on the one side of the two tablets of stone, and the other on the other side. However, it is no longer, "Thou shalt not," but on the flying roll are written the curses, the awful curses against the transgressors of God's law which are now about to be put into execution. The roll is of immense size, and on it are the dreadful curses of an angry God. The vision must have been one of exceeding great terror. Imagine a roll, probably illuminated at night with fire, moving over the heavens and on it the curses of an eternal God – wherever it moves its awful message is seen.

It reminds one of the fiery handwriting on the wall in the king's palace, as seen in Daniel 5:25. Surely such an awful judgment is coming by and by, when our God will keep silence no longer. The flying roll stands undoubtedly in connection with wickedness, theft and false swearing, as it is found in so many forms in unbelieving Israel. But it finds also a larger application in the judgment of wickedness throughout the earth on the glorious day of His appearing. This judgment will consume as per Malachi 3:2: "But who may abide the day of his coming? And who shall stand when he appeareth? For he is like a refiner's fire, and like fullers' soap:" At the second coming, God's fire will fall from heaven to consume the wood, hay and stubble. Nothing will be hid! Oh, what a burning that Day of the Lord will be when mankind's well-earned curses will be carried out in such a thorough way that none of the wicked can escape.

The Woman and the Ephah (5:5-11)

The next vision is one of great interest and not a little difficulty. In it we see again wickedness and judgment. Let's read the heart of it in Zechariah 5:7-11:

And, behold, there was lifted up a talent of lead: and this is a woman that sitteth in the midst of the ephah. And he said, This is wickedness. And he cast it into the midst of the ephah; and he cast the weight of lead upon the mouth thereof. Then lifted I up mine eyes, and looked, and, behold, there came out two women, and the wind was in their wings; for they had wings like the wings of a stork: and they lifted up the ephah between the earth and the heaven. Then said I to the angel that talked with me, Whither do these bear the ephah? And he said unto me, To build it an house in the land of Shinar: and it shall be established, and set upon her own base.

An ephah is a basket capable of holding up to 20 quarts – it is a measure used for the grain offering. It is used here as a Jewish measure standing here for commerce. The eyes of all the earth are upon it. Commercialism is very prominent in Revelation in connection with the fullness of wickedness, the climax of ungodliness.

In Revelation 18 merchants are mentioned who have grown rich though the abundances of her delicacies. Then the merchants are seen weeping, for no man buys their merchandise anymore. Then a long list follows, including all the articles of modern commerce. They show us that the climax of wickedness as it is in the earth when judgement will come and Israel's time commences once more, will be connected with commerce, riches and luxuries. The ephah points to this.

In the second place let us notice that in the midst of the ephah there is seen a woman who is called "wickedness." She has surrounded herself with the ephah and sits in the midst of it (Zech 5:7). Have we not here the great whore having a golden cup in her hand full of abominations and filthiness of her fornication? (Rev 17:4) Undoubtedly this woman is the type of evil and wickedness in its highest form. Is she not reminiscent of that woman in Revelation? She is the great whore sitting upon many waters as described in Revelation 17:3-6, who sits upon:

. . . a scarlet colored beast, full of names of blasphemy, having seven heads and ten horns. And the woman was arrayed in purple and scarlet colour, and decked with gold and precious stones and pearls, having a golden cup in her hand full of abominations and filthiness of her fornication: And upon her forehead was a name written, MYSTERY BABYLON THE GREAT, THE MOTHER OF HARLOTS AND ABOMINATIONS OF THE EARTH. And I saw the woman drunken with the blood of the saints, and with the blood of the martyrs of Jesus: and when I saw her, I wondered with great admiration.

The woman in the ephah resembles the same great whore, Babylon the great. This becomes at once clear when we take into consideration that the woman in the ephah is carried swiftly away and a house is built for her in the land of Shinar. Near the land of Shinar is Babylonia. This is where the God-opposing power has its home and where it will end in final and total destruction.

The first city erected after the flood was BABEL in the plain of Shinar (Gen 10:10). There they built a city and in it a tower, whose top was to reach into the heavens to make themselves a name (Gen 11:2-4). Self-worship had reached its climax at the Tower of Babel, and confusion and judgment came swiftly. The Babylon of the Revelation is the very same attempt, only in its fullest development. Thus we see in this vision of the ephah and the woman the overthrow and judgment of wickedness, with Babylon fallen, cast down. The Antichrist, the man of sin, will be slain by the brightness of his coming (2 Thess 2:8). Satan will be chained in the pit for a 1,000 years (Rev 20:2-4). The sixth vision of Zechariah is a vision of judgment upon the seat of Antichrist's global power in Babylon the great, the mother of harlots and abominations in the earth (Rev 17:5)

How do we get "there" from "here"? First, there will be the failure of the nation state. How does that happen? It begins when wealth and power become concentrated in the hands of a few and for the benefit of the few. The rich and powerful are not content to loot entire nations. They want to loot a collection of nations.

This leads inevitably to regionalism. The first such regional government in modern times is the European Union. What began in the 1950s as a trade agreement between a few European countries, has led to a comprehensive union among 28 European countries. The EU has a centralized government, a single currency and open borders between the member states. For all extents and purposes, it is a single country. The EU is a model for the regionalization of the world, into ten regions. This regionalization is predicted in Daniel 7:7, which states:

> After this I saw in the night visions, and behold a fourth beast, dreadful and terrible and strong exceedingly; and it had great iron teeth: it devoured and brake in pieces, and stamped the residue with the feet of it: and it was diverse from all the beasts that were before it; and it had ten horns.

These ten "horns" or regions are all at various stages of development presently and will eventually combine into one world government, or as globalist leaders call it, "The New World Order."[21] We read of this in Daniel 7:19-21:

---

21 In 1974, the Club of Rome (COR) divided the world into ten regions that will one day merge into a one world government. The COR has been assigned the task of overseeing the regionalization and unification of the entire world, where all nations of the world will give up their sovereignty in favor of a global government. The data regarding these regions is contained in the following book: M. Mesarovic and E. Pestel, *Mankind at the Turning Point-The Second Report to the Club of Rome*, E.P. Dutton & Co., Inc, Reader's Digest Press, 1974.

Then I would know the truth of the fourth beast, which was diverse from all the others, exceeding dreadful, whose teeth were of iron and his nails of brass; which devoured, brake in pieces, and stamped the residue with his feet; And of the ten horns that were in his head, and of the other which came up, and before whom three fell; even of that horn that had eyes, and a mouth that spake very great things, whose look was more stout than his fellows. I beheld, and the same horn made war with the saints, and prevailed against them:

This one world government will be followed by judgment at the second coming of Christ. We read of this in Daniel 7:22, "Until the Ancient of days came and judgment was given to the saints of the most High; and the time came that the saints possessed the kingdom."

THE FOUR CHARIOTS (6:1-8)

This is the last of the night visions given to the prophet Zechariah. In this vision the prophet lifts up his eyes again and sees four chariots which come out from between two mountains which were of brass. In the first chariot the horses are red; in the second they are black, in the third white, and in the fourth a dappled or speckled bay. The angel explains that these are the four spirits of the heaven which go forth from standing before the Lord of all the earth. The black and the white horse go forth into the north country, the speckled goes to the south county, and the bay went forth and sought to go so that they might walk to and fro through the earth. The last verse of the vision reads: "Then cried he upon me, and spake unto me, saying, Behold, these that go toward the north country have quieted my spirit in the north country."

We notice first the similarity to this last vision with the first vision contained in the opening chapter of Zechariah. The visions open with the hosts of heaven upon red, speckled and white horses, having walked to and fro through the earth. We learned from the first vision that its meaning was judgment; that God was displeased with the nations, and is once more jealous for Jerusalem and ready to turn in mercy to Zion, and the hosts of heaven are seen in that first vision preparing for judgment. In the last vision the chariots of judgment are seen coming forth to sweep over the earth, to be followed by the crowning with crowns of the high priest. The riders of the first vision may be termed the advance guards of the judgment, but the chariots now put the divine decrees into action.

The riders halted in a valley amidst a myrtle grove, but the chariots rush forth to execute their terrible work from between two mountains of brass. These mountains probably refer to Mount Moriah and the Mount of Olives. These chariots rush through the Valley of Jehoshaphat. The brass is mentioned to denote the firmness and stability of these mountains, which have never been moved. The judgment of them is now come. The stone is falling and smiting the image at its feet and pulverizing it, putting it completely out of existence. The chariots are God's powers, agencies for judgment in the earth, which will pass swiftly along, shown by the fast running chariots. In Revelation six the seven seals are opened, and there go forth the four terrible riders upon white, red, black and pale horses. The riders in the Apocalypse are the riders which go through the earth following the Rapture, but in the last night vision of Zechariah we see the chariots of God's wrath.

The vision falls in the time when heaven opens and He appears riding upon a white horse, His name Faithful and True, coming in righteousness to judge and make war. This is a wonderful vision of Him who is clothed with a vesture dipped in blood! He is followed by the armies of heaven upon white horses, all clothed in fine linen white and clean (Rev 19:11-14)

In summary, the final night vision of Zechariah will be fulfilled during the Tribulation as God's wrath is poured out on the world. This will conclude when the heavens open and Christ appears riding upon a white horse, coming in righteousness to judge and make war (Rev 19:11). As believers, how our hearts should rejoice and praise our God who has delivered us from that wrath to come (1 Thess 5:9). The time is short, and soon the scenes of terror, Tribulation and God's wrath will be enacted in the earth. The removal of the Church from the earth will greatly accelerate deteriorating world events, leading to the beginning of this dreaded time.

CHAPTER 7

Prophecies About Christ's First Coming

§

As we begin to look at the specific predictions concerning the first coming of Christ, keep in mind that the book of Zechariah was written during the time period of approximately 520-480 B.C., about half a millennia before the incarnation of Christ. Throughout the balance of the book, we will be considering these prophecies in the chronological order in which they have been or will be fulfilled. It is truly an amazing testimony of the divine authorship of these prophecies when we consider the exactitude in which they were fulfilled.

His Humanity

The first amazing prophecy we will consider in reference to Christ's first coming has to do with statements concerning His humanity. Zechariah 6:12 states:

> And speak unto him saying, Thus speaketh the LORD of hosts saying, Behold the man whose name is the BRANCH; and he shall grow up out of his place, and he shall build the temple of the LORD.

Jeremiah predicted the coming of "the Branch of righteousness" in 33:15: "In those days, and at that time, will I cause the Branch of righteousness to grow up unto David; and he shall execute judgment and righteousness in the land." Echoing Jeremiah's prediction, Zechariah speaks of "the man whose name is the BRANCH" who will come to occupy David's throne and to build the millennial temple. Notice that this verse declares the humanity of Christ:

"Behold the man!" Christ is the perfect man as well as being fully God. We learn in Psalm 8:6 that God made Adam, before his fall ". . . to have dominion over the works of thy hands; thou hast put all things under his feet." In Christ, the second Adam, God's original intention in the creation is fulfilled. He is the new Adam, the Messianic King, who will have dominion over the whole world.

His Priesthood

Not only will the man whose name is THE BRANCH come to occupy David's throne and build the millennial temple, but He will also be a priest. This is seen in Zechariah 6:13-14:

> Even he shall build the temple of the LORD; and he shall bear the glory, and shall sit and rule upon his throne: and he shall be a priest upon his throne: and the counsel of peace shall be between them both. And the crowns shall be to Helem, and to Tobijah, and to Jedaiah, and to Hen the son of Zephaniah, for a memorial in the temple of the LORD.

Not only will the Messianic Branch build the temple, but He will also have regal splendor, will take His seat on His throne and rule, and will perfectly combine the two offices of king and priest. "His throne" is a reference to the promised Davidic throne as promised in 2 Samuel 7:16: "And thine house and thy kingdom shall be established for ever before thee: thy throne shall be established forever." King David also predicted one who would be "a priest forever" in Psalm 110:4: "The Lord hath sworn, and will not repent, Thou art a priest forever after the order of Melchizedek."

The BRANCH will come to occupy David's throne and will build the millennial temple. But He will also be "a priest forever," our eternal Priest-King. Joshua would build the post-exilic restoration temple, along with Zerubbabel, and this becomes a type of Christ as both priest and king. The crowns themselves were to be laid up in the temple as a memorial as seen in Zechariah 6:14: "And the crowns shall be to Helem, and to Tobijah, and to Jedaiah, and to Hen the son of Zephaniah, for a memorial in the temple of the LORD." It was to keep the Messianic hope alive that the crown was made for Joshua's symbolic crowning and then placed in the temple as a reminder of this hope.

His Deity

Not only does Zechariah speak of Christ's humanity and His priesthood, but he also speaks forthrightly concerning Christ's deity. We read in Zechariah 13:6, 7:

> And one shall say unto him, What are these wounds in thine hands? Then he shall answer, Those with which **I was wounded** in the house of my friends. Awake, O sword, against my shepherd, and **against the man that is my fellow**, saith the LORD of hosts: smite the shepherd, and the sheep shall be scattered: and I will turn mine hand upon the little ones (emphasis added).

This passage brings together both the humanity and deity of the Lord Jesus Christ. His humanity is clearly revealed in the statement regarding the wounds in His hands. Not only had His side been pierced, but also His hands (Ps 22:16), and these wounds remained even in His resurrected body (John 20:24-26). With great sadness, Christ states that these everlasting wounds had been inflicted at the urging of those who should have been His friends, the nation He had come to redeem.

The statement regarding the smiting of the shepherd is quoted by Christ Himself in Matthew 26:31 on the night of His betrayal: "Then saith Jesus unto them, All ye shall be offended because of me this night: for it is written, I will smite the shepherd, and the sheep of the flock shall be scattered abroad." Christ, the Good Shepherd, would give His life for the sheep (John 10:11) but, in the trauma of these world-changing events, His sheep would be scattered for a while. This was true, in the short term, of Christ's disciples. It was also true, in the larger sense, of the nation Israel, which was scattered in A.D. 70.

Not only is Christ's humanity declared in these verses, but His deity as well. Notice that the Lord of hosts declares that Jesus Christ is "the man that is my fellow." Here the Lord God makes the amazing statement that this Coming One whom He Himself would smite, is of equal status with God the Father! There is no stronger statement in the Old Testament regarding the unimpeachable deity of Christ, as Israel's smitten Shepherd.

His Triumphal Entry

As we transition from the person of Christ to the work of Christ in His first coming, we begin by looking at Zechariah 9:9, which deals with Christ's triumphant entry into Jerusalem, on what is commonly known as Palm Sunday:

Rejoice greatly, O daughter of Zion; shout, O daughter of Jerusalem; behold thy King coming unto thee; he is just, and having salvation; lowly, and riding upon an ass, and upon a colt, the foal of an ass.

Note the characteristics ascribed to this coming King. First, He is *just*, or righteous. Justice is the most important prerequisite for His office as king, as justice is basic to true world peace. The quality of justice is a characteristic of the ideal king. We read of this in 2 Samuel 23:3: ". . . He that ruleth over men must be just, ruling in the fear of God."

Secondly, He brings *salvation*, for justice is of little benefit to one whose life is not right with God. This word "saving" could either have the idea of "having salvation," or it could have the meaning of "showing Himself a Saviour-Deliverer."

The third characteristic is that He is *lowly*. In contrast to most kings, He is humble. Jesus speaks of this inherent quality in Matthew 11:29:

"Take my yoke upon you, and learn of me: for I am meek and lowly in heart: and ye shall find rest unto you souls." He comes in lowliness.

The fourth characteristic is *peacefulness*. This is suggested in His riding on a colt, the foal of a donkey, rather than astride a war horse. Christ, in His role as our suffering Savior, came the first time in a lowly, peaceful fashion, riding on an ass, rather than coming on a white horse at His second coming in power and glory (Rev 19:11).

Although Jesus was acclaimed Messiah at His triumphal entry into Jerusalem, His own people nevertheless rejected Him and the peace He came to offer. S. Lewis Johnson captures the significance of the scene:

Because they will not have Him at His first coming in peace, peace shall flee from them. Seeing the future discipline and chastening of the nation, He wept. Walking headlong to ruin, they shall have to learn the sad lesson that the triumphal entry was not only the story of the nation's rejection of its King, but also of their King's rejection of them. Yet, all is not lost. The future holds a glorious hope. The promises, unconditioned in their ultimate fulfillment, shall be realized. Israel may deny Him, crucify Him and attempt to forget Him; but His word is inviolate. Disobedience may thwart the enjoyment of the promises, but it cannot cancel title to them or the ultimate possession of them. The day is coming, as He Himself suggested a few days later, when Israel in full understanding shall shout the acclamation again, as they see Him coming the second time for deliverance: "Blessed is he that cometh in the name of the Lord" (cf. Matt 23:37-39). Then shall take place the entry that is really triumphal (cf. Zech 14:1-11). In the meantime, their house, as history has proved, is desolate.[22]

An interesting side note is seen in the next verse, Zechariah 9:10:

> And I will cut off the chariot from Ephraim, and the horse from Jerusalem, and the battle bow shall be cut off: and he shall speak peace unto the heathen: and his dominion shall be from sea even to the sea, and from the river even to the ends of the earth.

The lowly King, who came the first time riding on an ass, will eventually cause all wars to cease and will become ruler over all the earth, from sea to sea. This obviously did not happen when He came fulfilling the first part of this prophecy, entering Jerusalem on a young donkey. As with numerous prophecies, especially Messianic prophecies, there is a blending of the events of His first and second coming.

An illustration of this is that of an observer looking at two far-off mountain ranges. Unaware that there is a great valley between the ranges, he assumes that they are part of the same mountain range, describing the two together. However, the mountain ranges may be separated by a great distance. Likewise, Zechariah 9:9, 10 has features that are descriptive of the Lord's first and second coming, events that are separated by nearly two thousand years at present.

The Apostle Peter acknowledged the fascination biblical prophets had with the distance between the two comings of Christ. We read of this in 1 Peter 1:10, 11:

---

22 S.L. Johnson, "The Triumphal Entry of Christ," *Bibliotheca Sacra* 124 (July-September 1967) 228-29.

Of which salvation the prophets have enquired and searched diligently, who prophesied of the grace *that should come* unto you: Searching what, or what manner of time the Spirit of Christ which was in them did signify, when it testified beforehand the sufferings of Christ, and the glory that should follow.

We see from this passage the historic fascination and inquiry by God's prophets regarding the span of time between Christ's first coming, which was characterized by *sufferings*, and Christ's second coming, which will be characterized by *glory*. Earnest students of Bible prophecy continue to be fascinated with this subject.

Another example of how these two "mountain peaks of prophecy" are brought together in Scripture is found in Isaiah 61:1, 2a:

The Spirit of the Lord God is upon me; because the LORD hath anointed me to preach good tidings unto the meek; he hath sent me to bind up the broken-hearted, to proclaim liberty to the captives, and the opening of the prison to them that are bound; To proclaim the acceptable year of the Lord, and the day of vengeance of our God.

In this passage, elements of both the first and second coming of Christ are brought together without grammatical interruption. Notice how Jesus carefully quoted from this passage in such a way as to *create* an interruption. When Jesus was visiting his boyhood home in Nazareth he stood up in the synagogue and read from the prophet Isaiah:

The Spirit of the Lord is upon me, because he hath anointed me to preach the gospel to the poor; he hath sent me to heal

the brokenhearted, to preach deliverance to the captives, and
recovering of sight to the blind, to set at liberty them that are
bruised, To preach the acceptable year of the Lord'. And he
closed the book . . . and he began to say unto them, 'This day is
this scripture fulfilled in your ears' (Luke 4:18-21).

Jesus knew exactly where to stop quoting Isaiah's prophecy to include
only that which pertained to His first coming, as only that portion of
the prophecy was being fulfilled at that time. He omitted the phrase
". . . and the day of vengeance of our God . . ." (Is 61:2b). So, as we
consider the Messianic prophecies in Zechariah, we must keep in mind
that, on occasion, prophecies concerning the first and second coming
of Christ are brought together without grammatical interruption.

Before leaving the subject of the triumphal entry, one additional
observation pertains to the timing of that event. Sir Robert Anderson,
in his classic book *The Coming Prince* painstakingly demonstrates that
exactly 69 "weeks" (483 years) transpired between the decree of Cyrus
and the Triumphal Entry, in fulfillment of Daniel 9:25, 26. This will
be expanded on in our next chapter. Thus, God is never early or late in
fulfilling Bible prophecy, but is always right on time.[23]

---

23 Robert Anderson, *The Coming Prince* (Grand Rapids: Kregel, 19th edition, 1975)
119-129.

His Betrayal

The next prophecy that occurs in the life of Christ is His betrayal, as recorded in Zechariah 11:12, 13:

> And I said unto them, if ye think good, give me my price; and if not, forbear. So they weighed for my price thirty pieces of silver. And the Lord said unto me, Cast it unto the potter—a lordly price that I was prized at of them. And I took the thirty pieces of silver, and cast them to the potter in the house of the Lord.

The speaker in this passage is Christ Himself, and He is asking for the Jew's evaluation of His labors and His worth. Their appraisal amounted to the price of an ox-gored slave. We read of that in Exodus 21:32: "If the ox shall push a manservant or a maidservant; he shall give unto their master thirty shekels of silver, and the ox shall be stoned."

The betrayal of Jesus, the Son of God, for thirty pieces of silver, is one of the most ludicrous transactions reported in the Bible. Far worse than outright rejection, the Jewish readers placed the Lord Jesus Christ on the value level of an injured slave. The remarkable accuracy and detail of this prophecy is shown not only by the disclosure of the exact amount of "blood money" given, but also by the fact that it would be thrown down in the House of the Lord by the conscience-stricken Judas, and that the money would be used to purchase the potter's field to bury Judas. We read of the fulfillment of this amazing prophecy in Matthew 26:14-16; 27:3-8:

Then one of the twelve, called Judas Iscariot, went unto the chief priests, And said unto them, What will ye give me, and I will deliver him unto you? And they covenanted with him for thirty pieces of silver. And from that time he sought opportunity to betray him . . . Then Judas, which had betrayed him, when he saw that he was condemned, repented himself, and brought again the thirty pieces of silver to the chief priest and elders, Saying, I have sinned in that I have betrayed the innocent blood. And they said, What is that to us? See thou to that. And he cast down the pieces of silver in the temple, and departed, and went and hanged himself. And the chief priests took the silver pieces, and said, It is not lawful for to put them into the treasury, because it is the price of blood. And they took counsel, and bought with them the potter's field, to bury strangers in. Wherefore that field was called, The field of blood, unto this day.

THE SMITTEN SHEPHERD

After the betrayal, Christ is tortured and eventually crucified. The book of Zechariah predicts that as well. We read in Zechariah 13:7:

Awake, O sword, against my shepherd, and against the man who is my fellow, saith the Lord of hosts; smite the shepherd and the sheep shall be scattered; and I will turn mine hand upon the little ones.

There are many truths to be drawn from this rich prophetic verse. First, we note that this smiting or crucifixion is viewed as an act of the Father, something which God Himself ordained and controlled. Christ acknowledged this fact in the Garden of Gethsemane, when He prayed, "nevertheless, not my will, but thine, be done" (Luke 22:42). Peter echoes the same thing when he thundered to the assembled Jews on the Day of Pentecost in Acts 2:22, 23:

> Ye men of Israel, hear these words; Jesus of Nazareth a man approved of God among you by miracles, and wonders and signs, which God did by him in the midst of you, as ye yourselves also know: Him, being delivered by the determinate counsel and foreknowledge of God, ye have taken and by wicked hands have crucified and slain.

Notice the seamless blending of divine sovereignty and human responsibility. On the one hand, Peter declares that the crucifixion of the Son of God was accomplished by "the determinate counsel and foreknowl-edge of God." In other words, the suffering and slaying of the second member of the Godhead did not take God the Father by surprise. In the eternal counsel of God, before the world was created or the fall of man, it was ordained that Christ must suffer and die on behalf of the sins of man. He was truly ". . . the lamb slain from the foundation of the world" (Rev 13:8).

At the same time, Peter emphasized the human responsibility of those who put Christ to death. He declared unequivocally to the Jews assembled in Jerusalem: ". . . ye have taken, and by wicked hands have crucified and slain" (Acts 2:23). In other words, even though the cru-cifixion of Christ had been worked out in the eternal counsel of the Godhead, there was still culpability on the part of those who actually carried out that plan. Hence, divine sovereignty and human responsi-bility stand side by side.

Though divine sovereignty and human responsibility appear to be an *antinomy*, that is, a law which seems to contradict itself, it is, in reality, not a contradiction in the plan of God. *Webster's New World Dictionary* defines an antinomy as "a contradiction or inconsistency between two apparently reasonable principles or laws."[24] For our purposes, however, this definition is not quite accurate; the opening words should read "an *appearance* of a contradiction . . ." Both divine sovereignty and human responsibility came into play in the smiting of the Shepherd.

Secondly, as noted previously, God addresses Christ as "His fellow," denoting an equality of being. If Christ is referred to as the "fellow" of the Lord of hosts, then Christ must be of the same nature and status as God the Father. This concept of perfect equality between God the

---

24 *Webster's New World Dictionary of the American Language* (NY: The World Publishing Company,1970) 60.

Father and God the Son is expressed many times in the New Testament. A classic expression of that equality is found in Philippians 2:5-8:

> Let this mind be in you, which was also in Christ Jesus: Who, being in the form of God, thought it not robbery to be equal with God: But made himself of no reputation, and took upon him the form of a servant, and was made in the likeness of men: and being found in fashion as a man, he humbled himself, and became obedient unto death, even the death of the cross.

Thirdly, this verse prophesies about the Roman general Titus, who led a two-year siege, culminating in the sacking of Jerusalem. Flavius Josephus describes some of the suffering experienced by the Jews in Jerusalem during this siege:

> Now of those that perished by famine in the city, the number was prodigious, and the miseries they underwent were unspeakable; for if so much as the shade of any kind of food did anywhere appear, a war was commenced presently; and the dearest friends fell a-fighting one with one another about it, snatching from each other the most miserable supports of life. Nor would men believe that those who were dying had no food; but the robbers would search them when they were expiring, lest any one would have concealed food in their bosoms, and counterfeited dying: nay, these robbers gaped for want, and ran about stumbling and staggering along like mad dogs, and reeling against the doors of the houses like drunken men; they would also, in the great distress they were in, rush into the very same houses two or three times in one and the same day. Moreover, their hunger was so intolerable, that it obliged them to chew everything while they

gather such things as the most sordid animals would not touch and endured to eat them; nor did they at length abstain from girdles and shoes; and the very leather which belonged to their shield they pulled off and gnawed.[25]

Thus, Josephus goes into great detail as to the manner in which the sheep were scattered as a consequence of Israel's smiting of the Shepherd. We have seen in this chapter that there are many prophecies in the Book of Zechariah that pertain to the first coming of Christ. All of these prophecies were fulfilled in a literal way, and in great detail. This should be instructive to us in terms of the manner in which we should expect the prophecies in Zechariah that pertain to the second coming of Christ to be fulfilled. We should, therefore, have great confidence that we can obtain an accurate interpretation of those yet unfulfilled prophecies pertain to Christ's second coming and the establishment of His millennial kingdom. After an extended treatment of the timing of the Triumphal Entry in the next chapter, we will then proceed to examine prophecies that pertain to Christ's second coming.

---

25 Josephus, *The Works of Josephus.* Translated by William Whiston (Lynn, MA: Hendrickson Publishers, 1980) 578.

CHAPTER 8

The Timing of The Triumphal Entry

§

IN THE LAST CHAPTER, WE began to look at the specific predictions concerning the first coming of Christ. We looked at prophecies concerning His humanity, His priesthood, His deity, His triumphal entry, His

betrayal, His sufferings and the dispersion of Israel. In this chapter, we are going to look in more depth at the timing of the triumphal entry. This will be a fascinating study that will attest to the inerrancy and accuracy of the Word of God. Let's begin by reviewing the prophecy concerning the triumphal entry in Zechariah 9:9:

> Rejoice greatly, O daughter of Zion; shout, O daughter of Jerusalem; behold thy King coming unto thee; he is just, and having salvation; lowly, and riding upon an ass, and upon a colt, the foal of an ass.

The fulfillment of that prophecy is found in both Matthew 21:1-5 and John 12:14, 15. The Matthew 21 passage reads as follows:

> And when they drew nigh unto Jerusalem, and were come to Bethphage, unto the mount of Olives, then sent Jesus two disciples, Saying unto them, Go into the village over against you, and straightway ye shall find an ass tied, and a colt with her: loose them, and bring them unto me. And if any man say ought unto you, ye shall say, The Lord hath need of them; and straightway he will send them. All this was done, that it might be fulfilled which was spoken by the prophet, saying, Tell ye the daughter of Sion, Behold, thy King cometh unto thee, meek, and sitting upon an ass, and a colt the foal of an ass.

Here in Matthew's gospel the inspired author quotes from Zechariah 9:9 claiming these events he witnessed were the fulfillment of Zechariah's prophesy. In this chapter we are going to demonstrate that exactly 69 "weeks" or 483 prophetic years transpired between the decree of Cyrus and the triumphal entry, in exact fulfillment of Bible prophecy.

To begin to address the issue of the timing of the triumphal entry, we must examine the prophecy known as "Daniel's 70th week" as found in Daniel 9:24-27:

> Seventy weeks are determined upon thy people, and upon thy holy city, to finish the transgression, and to make an end of sins, and to make reconciliation for iniquity, and to bring in ever-lasting righteousness, and to seal up the vision and prophecy and to anoint the most Holy. Know therefore and understand, that from the going forth of the commandment to restore and

to build Jerusalem unto the Messiah the Prince shall be seven weeks, and threescore and two weeks: the street shall be built again, and the wall, even in troublous times. And after three-score and two weeks shall Messiah be cut off, but not for him-self: and the people of the prince that shall come shall destroy the city and the sanctuary; and the end thereof shall be with a flood, and unto the end of the war desolations are determined. And he shall confirm the covenant with many for one week: and in the midst of the week he shall cause the sacrifice and the oblation to cease, and for the overspreading of abominations he shall make it desolate, even until the consummation, and that determined shall be poured upon the desolate.

This prophecy of Daniel's 70 weeks is critical to understanding Bible prophecy as it relates to the nation Israel. While Daniel had been med-itating on God's promise that the Babylonian captivity would be 70 years, Gabriel brought to him the message that not just 70 years, but 70 "sevens of years," were determined on his people. That is, God would be dealing with Israel's covenant people for a period of 70 weeks of years, or 490 years, though not 490 contiguous years. There would be an indeterminate gap between the 69th and 70th week.

The events prophesied for these 490 years are critical for the proper understanding of eschatology and prophecy. Furthermore, the remark-able fulfillment of the key portions of the prophecy of the 70 weeks is certainly one of the strongest evidences for the supernatural inspira-tion of Scripture. Let's begin to unpack this prophecy as it relates to the timing of the triumphal entry.

This prophecy deals with a time period that eventuates with the cutting off of the Messiah (9:26). Many believe the cutting off of the Messiah actually took place on the day of the triumphal entry. The blessings promised to Judah and Jerusalem were postponed until after a period described as the "seventy weeks;" and at the close of the 69th week of years (483 years) the Messiah should be "cut off."

These 70 weeks represent 490 prophetic years of 360 days, to be reckoned from the issuing of an edict regarding the rebuilding of the city of Jerusalem. The edict in question was the decree issued by Artaxerxes Longimanus in the twentieth year of his reign, authorizing Nehemiah to rebuild the fortifications of Jerusalem (cf. Neh 2:1-8). The date of Artaxerxes' reign can be definitely ascertained – not just from prophetic writers such as Nehemiah, but by the united voice of secular historians and chronologers. The statement of Luke 3:1 is explicit and unequivocal, that our Lord's public ministry began in the fifteenth year of Tiberius Caesar. The date of it can thus be fixed between August A.D. 28 and April A.D. 29. The Passover of the crucifixion therefore was in A.D. 32, when Christ was betrayed on the night of the Paschal Supper, and put to death on the day of the Paschal Feast.

If then the forgoing conclusions be well founded, we should expect to find that the period intervening between the edict of Artaxerxes and the Passion was 483 prophetic years. A prophetic year is made up of 360 days. If God has deigned to mark on human calendars the fulfilment of His purposes as foretold in prophecy, the strictest scrutiny shall fail to detect miscalculation or mistake.

The Persian edict which restored the autonomy of Judah was issued in the Jewish month of Nisan. It may in fact have been dated the 1st of Nisan, but no other day being named the prophetic period must be reckoned, according to a practical common with the Jews, from the Jewish New Year's Day. The seventy weeks are therefore to be computed from the 1st of Nisan B.C. 445.

Now the great characteristic of the Jewish sacred year has remained unchanged ever since the memorable night when the equinoctial moon beamed down upon the hosts of Israel in Egypt. There is no doubt or difficulty in fixing with narrow limits the Julian Calendar date of the 1st of Nisan in any year whatever. In B.C. 445 the new moon by which the Passover was regulated was on the 13th of March. And accordingly the 1st of Nisan may be assigned to the 14th of March.

The language of the prophecy is clear: "Know therefore and understand, that from the going forth of the commandment to restore and to build Jerusalem unto the Messiah the Prince shall be seven weeks, and threescore and two weeks" (9:25). An era of 69 weeks of years, or 483 prophetic years reckoned from the 14th of March, B.C. 445, should close with some event to satisfy the words, "unto the Messiah the Prince."

The date of the nativity could not possibly have been the termination of the period, for then the 69 weeks must have ended 33 years before Messiah's death. If the beginning of His public ministry be fixed upon, difficulties of another kind present themselves. When the Lord began to preach, the kingdom was not presented as a fact accomplished in His advent, but as a hope, the realization of which, though at the very door, was still to be fulfilled. The ministry of Jesus was a preparation for the kingdom, leading up to the time when, in fulfillment of the prophetic Scriptures, He should publicly declare Himself as the Son of David, the King of Israel, and claim the homage of the nation. It was Israel's fault and guilt (though in the determinate counsel of God – Acts 2:23) that the cross and not the throne was the climax of His life on earth during His first advent.

It was the Lord's last visit to Jerusalem that was the crisis of His ministry, the goal towards which it had been directed. After the first tokens had been given that the nation would reject His Messianic claims, He had shunned all public recognition of them. But now the twofold testimony of His words and His works had been fully rendered and His entry into the Holy City was to proclaim His Messiahship and to receive His doom.

Again and again His apostles had been charged that they should not make Him known. But now, at His triumphal entry, He accepted the acclamations of the whole multitude of His followers, and silenced the opposition of the Pharisees with the indignant rebuke, "I tell you if these should hold their peace, the stones would immediately cry out" (Luke 19:39, 40).

As the shouts broke forth from His disciples, "Blessed be the King that cometh in the name of the Lord!" (Luke 19:38), He looked off toward the Holy City and exclaimed, "If thou also hadst known, even thou, at the least on this day, the things which belong unto thy peace! but now they are hid from thine eyes" (Luke 19:42).

The time of Jerusalem's visitation had come, and she knew it not. Long before this day the nation had rejected Him, but this was the predestined day when their choice must be irrevocable. This day so distinctly signaled in Scripture as the fulfilment of Zechariah's prophecy, "Rejoice greatly, O daughter of Zion; Shout, O daughter of Jerusalem; behold thy King cometh unto thee: he is just, and having salvation; lowly and riding upon an ass, and upon a colt the foal of an ass" (Zech 9:9). Of all the days of the ministry of Christ on earth, no other will satisfy so well the words "And after threescore and two weeks shall Messiah be cut off . . ." (Dan 9:25).

The date of the triumphal entry can be determined through careful calculation! In accordance with the Jewish custom, the Lord went up to Jerusalem upon the 8th Nisan, "six days before the Passover" (John 11:55). But as the 14th day of Nisan, on which the Paschal Supper was eaten, fell that year upon a Thursday, the 8th was the preceding Friday.

He must have spent the Sabbath, therefore, at Bethany; and on the evening of the 9th, after the Sabbath had ended, the Supper took place in Martha's house. Upon the following day, the 10th of Nisan, He entered Jerusalem as recorded Luke 19.

The date in the Julian Calendar of that 10th of Nisan was Sunday, the 6th of April, A.D. 32. What then was the length of the period intervening between the issuing of the decree to rebuild Jerusalem and the triumphal entry – between the 14th of March, B.C. 445, and the 6th of April, A.D. 32? The interval contained exactly to the very day, 173,880 days, or seven times 69 prophetic years (483 years) of Gabriel's prophecy found in Daniel 9:25.

The chart reproduced below comes from Sir. Robert Anderson's book, The Coming Prince:[26]

The 1st Nisan in the 20th year of Artaxerxes (the edict to rebuild Jerusalem) was 14th March, B.C. 445.

The 10th Nisan in Passion Week (Christ's entry into Jerusalem) was 6th April, A.D. 32.

The intervening period was 476 years and 24 days (the days being reckoned inclusively, as required by the language of the prophecy, and in accordance with the Jewish practice).

But 476 x 365 =	173,740 days
Add (14 March to 6th April)	+ 24
Add for leap years	+ 116
	173,880[27]

---

26 Robert Anderson, *The Coming Prince* (Grand Rapids: Kregel, 19th edition, 1975) 128.

27 It may be well to offer here two explanatory remarks. First: in reckoning years from B.C. to A.D., one year must always be omitted; for it is obvious . . . that from B.C. 1 to A.D. 1 was not two years, but one year. B.C. I ought to be described as B.C.

This number, 173,880 days, equals 483 prophetic years TO THE DAY! Let me conclude this chapter with the words of Sir Robert Anderson:

> Much there is in Holy Writ which unbelief may value and revere, while utterly refusing to accept it as Divine; but prophecy admits of no half-faith. The prediction of the "seventy weeks" was either a gross and impious imposture, or else it was in the fullest and strictest sense *God-breathed* . . . To believe that the facts and figures here detailed amount to nothing more than happy coincidence involves a greater exercise of faith than that of the Christian who accepts the book of Daniel as Divine. There is a point beyond which unbelief is impossible, and the mind in refusing truth must needs take refuge in a misbelief which is sheer credulity.[28]

"O" and it is so reckoned by astronomers, who would describe the historical date B.C. 445, as 444. And secondly, the Julian year is 11m. 10'46s, or about the 129th part of a day, longer than the mean solar year. The Julian calendar, therefore contains three leap years too many in four centuries, Ibid, 128.

28 Ibid, 129.

CHAPTER 9

Prophecies About Christ's Second Coming

§

WE HAVE SEEN THUS FAR in our study of the book of Zechariah that it contains scattered prophecies concerning the past pilgrimage of Christ upon this earth when He came to suffer and die for our sins. We will see in the last two chapters of our study that Zechariah abounds with prophecies concerning Israel's regathering in the latter days, and the events connected with the return and reign of the Messiah, the Lord Jesus Christ. In fact, this is the burden of chapters 9-14 of Zechariah. Due to the vast amount of scriptural data dealing with this future time, the focus of our study will be exclusively on those prophecies which specifically refer to Christ's second coming and His earthly millennial reign. We will deal with those prophecies in chronological order.

HIS ARRIVAL ON THE MOUNT OF OLIVES

The first prophecy in Zechariah that will be fulfilled at Christ's second coming is in regards to His arrival upon the Mount of Olives. We read about this in Zechariah 14:4:

And his feet shall stand in that day upon the Mount of Olives, which is before Jerusalem on the east, and the Mount of Olives shall cleave in the midst thereof toward the east and toward the west, and there shall be a very great valley; and half of the mountains shall remove toward the north and half of it toward the south.

This incredible prophecy is actually very credible, according to the modern science of seismography. For example, an article entitled, "Zechariah and the Rift Valley," states:

The Great Rift Valley is a unique topographical feature along which the ground has sunk between parallel faults. It extends north and south along the Jordan Valley, the Red Sea, and though Africa to the Zambezi River, in the southeast . . . Such tremendous topographical changes would be the result of a great earthquake along a unique fault line scarred with signs of earth movements. This fault line is regarded by seismologists as a region of great potential earthquake danger. The River Jordan runs north and south through a portion of this great fault in the earth's crusts. This fault begins in the Toros Mountains in Turkey, continues down the Jordan Valley, through the Gulf of Aqaba, across the Red Sea, and ends somewhere in southeast Africa. From its source in the mountain in Turkey the Jordan River flows southward over a distance of 240 miles, descending to a remarkable 1,209- feet below sea level where it reaches the Dead Sea. This is the lowest body of water on the surface of the earth.[29]

---

29 *Zechariah and the Rift Valley* (Christian Assemblies International: cal.org/biblestudies/zechariah), 1.

The Mount of Olives is around 2,600 feet above sea level. That means that the "cleaving" mentioned in Zechariah 14:4 would have to be at least 2,600 feet deep. You would have to add at least another 50 feet to that for the water to flow from the Mediterranean Sea to the Dead Sea, which is 1,300 feet below sea level (the lowest place on earth). Add to that fact is that this valley will have to run from Jerusalem to the Mediterranean Sea, about 40 miles. Then from Jerusalem to the Dead Sea is another 28 miles. Thus, we would have a valley caused by an earthquake that is at least 2,546 feet deep, and 68 miles long. There has never been an earthquake of this magnitude in recorded history! Zechariah 14:8 states: "And it shall be in that day, that living waters shall go out from Jerusalem; half of them towards the former sea (Mediterranean) and half of them towards the hinder sea (Dead Sea) in the summer and in the winter shall it be." Jerry Golden says in this regard:

> Now we see quite easily what is going to happen. The Messiah "Yeshua" on His return, will plant His feet on the Mount of Olives, and there will be an earthquake. It will cause the Mount of Olives to split even up to the Temple Mount. With the Mount of Olives split water will easily run to the Dead Sea, as it already runs to the Dead Sea through the Kidron Valley. With this water running from the Temple Mount it would have no problem finding its way to the Soreq River that runs near Bet Shemesh and into the Mediterranean Sea.[30]

---

30 J. Golden, "The Coming Earthquake on the Mount of Olives" (thegoldenreport. com. 2003) 1.

We find more Scripture on this subject in Ezekiel 47. We read in Ezekiel 47:1, 8, 10:

> Afterward he brought me again unto the door of the house; and behold, waters issued out from under the threshold of the house eastward: for the forefront of the house stood toward the east, and the waters came down from under the right side of the house, at the south side of the altar . . . Then said he unto me, These waters issue out toward the east country, and go down into the desert, and go into the sea: which being brought forth into the sea, the waters shall be healed. And it shall come to pass, that everything that liveth, which moveth, withersoever the rivers shall come, shall live: and there shall be a very great multitude of fish, because these waters shall come thither: for they shall be healed; and everything shall live whither the river cometh. And it shall come to pass, that the fishers shall stand upon it from Engedi even unto Enegiaim; they shall be a place to spread forth nets; their fish shall be according to their kinds, as the fish of the great sea, exceeding many.

This passage indicates that water will come out from under the "house," which is a reference to the "House of God" or Temple Mount. This passage also tells us that the waters of the Dead Sea will be healed. In fact, this healing will be so complete that there will be many fish and that fishermen will do very well fishing there. So the two seas will not run together. This will be fresh water and it will come from the Temple Mount. When you read Ezekiel 47 you will see it is no little stream but rather a great river. The following article details how the Dead Sea will be healed:

> In order for the Dead Sea to be healed it must be able to flow into the red Sea some 350 kilometers to the south at Eilat. And when you consider that the Dead Sea is the lowest place on the planet, at 1,300 feet below sea level, this means that Dead Sea must rise one way or another to sea level. That would also mean that the entire Jordan Valley would go under water, even the city of Tiberias in the north along with all the Kibbutz in that valley.[31]

Israel's National Repentance

At the crucifixion of Christ, the Jews present said, ". . . His blood be upon us, and on our children" (Matt 27:25). The Jewish people have carried the guilt and culpability of this horrendous crime for almost 2,000 years. They will continue to carry that guilt until the second coming of Christ. We read in Zechariah 12:10:

> And I will pour upon the house of David, and upon the inhabitants of Jerusalem, the Spirit of grace and of supplications; and

---

31 J. Golden, "The Coming Earthquake on the Mount of Olives" (thegoldenreport. com, 2003) 2.

they shall look upon me whom they have pierced, and they shall mourn for him, as one mourneth for his only son, and shall be in bitterness for him, as one that is in bitterness for his firstborn.

This verse reveals the anguish of the repentant Jews at the end of the Tribulation, as they realize that they have crucified the Messiah. This mourning will occur at Israel's National Day of Atonement in preparation for the establishment of the millennial kingdom. The Bible predicts that a godly remnant of one-third of Israel will be saved at that time. This is stated in Zechariah 13:8, 9:

And it shall come to pass, that in all the land, saith the Lord, two parts therein shall be cut off and die; but the third shall be left therein. And I will bring the third part through the fire, and will refine them as silver is refined, and will try them as gold is tried: they shall call on my name, and I will hear them: I will say, It is my people, and they shall say, The Lord is my God.

This remnant is comprised of the Jews that are commanded to flee at the midpoint of the tribulation when the abomination of desolation occurs. Jesus speaks of this in Matthew 24:15, 16:

When ye therefore shall see the abomination of desolation, spoken of by Daniel the prophet, stand in the holy place, (whoso readeth, let him understand): Then let them which be in Judaea flee into the mountains.

There are other passages of Scripture that speak of Israel's need for a "hiding place" during their time of Great Tribulation. For example, we read in Isaiah 26:20, 21:

Come, my people, enter thou into thy chambers, and shut thy doors about thee: hide thyself as it were for a little moment, until the indignation be overpast. For behold the Lord cometh out of his place to punish the inhabitants of the earth for their iniquity . . .

Many Bible scholars believe that Israel's hiding place will be the rock city of Petra in the land of Jordan. Let us consider some clues given in the Bible as to whether Petra will be this place of hiding. This list is condensed from *Petra in History and Prophecy*, by Noah Hutchings.[32]

Clue No. 1 – Accessibility: According to the prophecy of Jesus in the Olivet Discourse, the Jews will have to leave Jerusalem quickly after the abomination of desolation occurs. We read in Matthew 24:19-21:

And woe unto them that are with child, and to them that give suck in those days! But pray ye that your flight be not in the winter, neither on Sabbath day: For then shall be great tribulation, such as was not since the beginning of the world to this time, no, nor ever shall be.

Petra is approximately 120 miles southeast of Jerusalem in the Mount Seir mountains. This would be a three or four day journey by foot from Jerusalem. It is interesting to note that Jesus mentioned the hardships

---

32 Noah Hutchings, *Petra in History and Prophecy*, (Oklahoma City: Bible Belt Publishing, 2009), 148-158.

that would be involved in a winter flight. Winters in Jerusalem are not usually very severe, with temperatures normally in the 45 to 60 degree range. However, Petra is an entirely different climate; extremely hot in the summer and extremely cold in the winter. Jesus' warning about traveling in the winter is one indication that Petra will be Israel's place of refuge.

Clue No. 2 – Geography: Matthew 24:16 is very clear that the Jews are to "flee to the mountains." While Israel's highest point is 3,963

feet in elevation, their rolling hills would provide little in the way of protection. The highest mountains in Jordan are in Petra, and the rugged mountainous terrain there would provide ample protection for the Jewish remnant.

Clue No. 3 – Political: The hiding place of the Jews needs to be a place that would be difficult for the forces of Antichrist to reach. While the Antichrist, at the peak of his power, will have ". . . power . . . over all kindreds, and tongues and nations" (Rev 13:7), there will be one nation that will be released from Antichrist's control. We read in Daniel 11:41, ". . . but these shall escape out of his hand, even Edom, and Moab, and the chief of the children of Ammon."

The identity of this nation and its capital is not difficult to determine, as the boundaries of ancient Edom, Moab and Ammon form exactly the boundaries of modern Jordan. Also, the chief, or ruler, of Jordan will be living in the capital, Amman, just like Daniel prophesied.

Clue No. 4 – Availability: Next, let us consider just how big this hiding place will have to be in order for the Jewish remnant to hide there. If we can approximate the number of Jews that will be housed during the last three and one-half years of the tribulation, this will help us determine how large this hiding place will have to be.

We have already learned from Zechariah 13:8, 9 that only one-third of the Jews will be preserved until the end of the tribulation. There are approximately six million Jews in Israel today, so we must look for a location that will hide at least two million people. Petra is a vast complex of cave dwellings, covering approximately 20 square miles. Some of these dwellings can hold up to one thousand people. I have visited this rock city and it is immense! Plus, the city is practically empty of inhabitants currently, with the exception of a few Bedouins. Petra can easily hold two million people for a relatively short period of three and one half years.

Clue No. 5 – Scriptural: Psalm 60:1, 9-12 states plainly that after God has regathered Israel, they will have a time of great trouble, but the Lord will preserve them in the strong city of Edom.

> O God, thou has cast us off, thou hast scattered us, thou hast been displeased; O turn thyself to us again . . . who will bring me into the strong city? Who will lead me into Edom? Wilt not thou, O God, which hadst cast us off? And thou, O God, which didst not go out with our armies? Give us help from trouble: for vain is the help of man. Through God we shall do valiantly: for he it is that shall tread down our enemies.

We also read of Israel's hiding place in Isaiah 16:1: "Send ye the lamb to the ruler of the land from Sela to the wilderness, unto the mount of the daughter of Zion." The remainder of the chapter concerns Israel's hiding from the Antichrist in Moab and Edom and in verse 14 a specific period of "three years" is foretold: "But now the Lord hath spoken, saying, Within three years, as the years of an hireling, and the glory of

Moab shall be contemned, with all that great multitude; and the remnant shall be very small and feeble."

The Book of Revelation also provides us with some insights regarding this period in Israel's history. We read in Revelation 12:1-5:

> And there appeared a great wonder in heaven; a woman clothed with the sun, and the moon under her feet, and upon her head a crown of twelve stars: And she being with child cried, travailing in birth, and pained to be delivered. And there appeared another wonder in heaven; and behold a great red dragon, having seven heads and ten horns, and seven crowns upon his heads. And his tail drew the third part of the stars of heaven, and did cast them to the earth: and the dragon stood before the woman which was ready to be delivered, for to devour her child as soon as it was born. And she brought forth a man child, who was to rule all nations with a rod of iron; and her child was caught up unto God, and to his throne. And the woman fled into the wilderness, where she hath a place prepared to God, that they should feed her there a thousand two hundred and three score days (3 ½ years).

When the dragon (Satan) is cast out of Heaven, knowing that his defeat has been brought about by the elevation of the "Man-Child" to the place of power, he will concentrate his hatred on the "woman" (Israel) who gave Him birth. The woman will flee into the wilderness where she will be kept safe and nourished for three and a half years until the dragon is bound.

THE CITIES OF REFUGE
The "cities of refuge" of Old Testament times are a type of this "wilderness refuge" of the children of Israel during the latter half of the

tribulation. We read of the cities of refuge in Numbers 35:6: "And among the cities which ye shall give unto the Levites there shall be six cities for refuge, which ye shall appoint for the manslayer, that he may flee thither . . ." These cities of refuge were designated cities, three on each side of the River Jordan, where the "man slayer" could flee for safety from the "avenger of blood."

If it could be proved after trial that he had slain a man "willfully," the man slayer was turned over to the "avenger of blood." If the slaying was accidental, his life was spared, but he had to remain in the city of refuge until the death of the high priest. Three of these cities, selected by Moses, were on the east side of the Jordan: Bezer in Reuben; Ramoth-gilead in Gad; and Golan in Manasseh (Dt 4:41-43).

Later, under Joshua, the other three were named, being west of the Jordan: Kedesh in Naphtali; Shechem in Ephraim; and Hebron in Judah (Josh 20:7). These six cities were conveniently located in northern, central and southern areas of the land. Roads were to be built and kept open to these important cities (Deut 19:3).

Clarence Larkin speaks of the nation Israel as the "man slayer" in his excellent book, *Dispensational Truth*, originally published in 1920:

> Now if I find in the New Testament that a certain class of people are called upon to flee to a "Place of Refuge" for the protection of their lives, then I must believe that they flee because an "Avenger of Blood" is after them, and that they flee because they are guilty of "Manslaughter."
>
> Such a class of people I find in the Jewish race. They were the cause of the death of Christ, and though He was crucified by the Roman authorities they assumed the guilt for they cried— "His blood be on us, and on our children" (Mt 27:25). At first sight it looks like "willful" murder, yet from the prayer of Jesus

on the Cross—"Father, forgive them for they know not what they do," it is clear that Jesus' death was not so much a premeditated murder as it was a murder committed in blind religious frenzy. As Paul said, ". . . had they known they would not have crucified the Lord of glory" (1 Cor 2:8).

It is clear then that the Jewish race is only guilty of manslaughter. As the "Man-slayer" of Jesus, they have been for almost 1,800 years running for a "City of Refuge," and have not as yet reached it. The "Avenger of Blood" has been on their track and hounded them from nation to nation, and the epithet of "The Wandering Jews" has followed them down the centuries . . .[33]

If the Jews are the "man-slayers," who is the "avenger of blood?" Surely it is the Antichrist. If the "avenger of blood" must be a "Kinsman" of the man slain, that means that he must be of the same race, and the nearest kinsman alive at the time vengeance is sought. While Jesus was the first born of the Virgin Mary, he was not the only child she had. She afterward had by Joseph four sons that we know of—James, Joseph, Judah and Simon, as well as two daughters. Two of these brothers of Jesus occupied prominent roles in the early church. James was pastor of the church at Jerusalem, and Judas wrote the epistle of Jude.

The kinsfolk of Jesus can be traced as late as A.D. 324. Somewhere in the world today, without doubt, are living some of the relatives of the Lord Jesus. They may not be able to trace their descent back to Mary and Joseph, but God knows who they are and where they are. Could it be that when the time comes for the manifestation of the Antichrist, the

33 C. Larkin, *Dispensational Truth* (NY: republished by Cosimo Classics, 2008), 136-137.

"avenger of blood" will be a Jew who is a literal descendent of the family of Jesus?

As to the city of refuge that God will provide for Israel when the "avenger of blood" (the Antichrist), pursues Israel, we read in Isaiah 26:20, "Come, my people (Israel), enter thou into my chambers, and shut the doors about thee; hide thyself as it were for a little moment, until the indignation be overpast."

The context shows that this refers to the time when Antichrist, the "avenger of blood," will seek to destroy the Jewish people and is the time referred to by Christ in Matthew 24:15-22. Just as God took care of the children of Israel during their 40 years of wilderness wandering, it is in the same wilderness that God is going to provide for them a place of "refuge" in the day when the "avenger of blood" shall seek to destroy them.

Speaking of the Antichrist, the prophet Daniel says, "He shall enter also into the glorious land (Palestine) and many countries shall be overthrown; but these shall escape out of his hand, even Edom and Moab and the chief of the children of Ammon" (Dan 11:41). Edom takes in the wilderness where Israel wandered for 40 years. And it is here in Edom that the "city of refuge" that God has provided for Israel is located. When the time comes for the "man slayer" (Israel), to escape from the hands of the "avenger of blood" (Antichrist), the rocky vastness of the ancient city of Petra could very well be Israel's "city of refuge." It is here that Israel will be safe, until the return of the High Priest of Heaven, who as King-Priest of the armies of Heaven will deliver her and allow her to leave her place of refuge.

Thus, as we catch glimpses of the coming Christ in this chapter, we see that He will return on the Mount of Olives, causing a tremendous earthquake that will dramatically change the topography of Israel.

Then He will proceed to Petra, the "city of refuge" for Israel's remnant, where a great national day of repentance and redemption will take place. These events will set the stage for Christ's glorious millennial reign, which will be the subject of our next chapter.

CHAPTER 10

More Prophecies About Christ's Second Coming

§

IN THE PREVIOUS CHAPTER, WE began to look at prophecies pertaining
to the Lord's second coming. We looked at His arrival on the Mount of
Olives and considered the many geographical changes that will accompany that climactic event. We also looked at Israel's national repentance
that will take place when Christ appears to a remnant of Israel in their
"hiding place" in the mountains of Edom. In this chapter, we pick up
from there and consider the events that will take place as the Messiah
sets up His earthly millennial kingdom.

ISRAEL'S SPIRITUAL RESTORATION

After the Lord's coming in glory and the national repentance of Israel,
Zechariah promised the spiritual and material restoration of the Jewish

people. This spiritual restoration is promised in
Zechariah 13:1, 2:

> In that day there shall
> be a fountain opened to
> the house of David and
> to the inhabitants of
> Jerusalem for sin and for

uncleanness. And it shall come to pass in that day, saith the LORD of hosts, that I will cut off the names of the idols out of the land, they shall no more be remembered: and also I will cause the prophets and the unclean spirit to pass out of the land.

In symbolic language the Lord promises an outflowing of His Spirit on His covenant people. The imagery is doubtless that of water as an emblem of the Holy Spirit. The recipients are the leaders and people of Jerusalem, representative of the inhabitants of the whole land. The content of this outflowing is a "spirit of grace and supplication." Because of the convicting work of God's Spirit, Israel will turn to the Messiah with mourning. The repentance demonstrated in 12:10, 11 will bring forth, in chapter 13, worthy fruits of repentance. These fruits are the fulfillment of the terms of the New Covenant made with Israel in Jeremiah 31:33, 34:

> But this shall be the covenant that I will make with the house of Israel; After those days, saith the LORD, I will put my law in their inward parts, and write it in their hearts; and will be their God, and they shall be my people. And they shall teach no more every man his neighbor, and every man his brother, saying, Know the LORD: for they shall all know me, from the least of them unto the greatest of them, saith the LORD: for I will forgive their iniquity, and I will remember their sin no more.

In the New Covenant God promised Israel these provisions: (1) enablement through His Spirit to obey His law; (2) an intimate personal relationship and fellowship; (3) a saving knowledge of Himself; (4) the forgiveness of sins. These blessings will be experienced by a remnant of ethnic Israel at the second advent of the Messiah, thus preparing the priestly nation for the Lord's service. Paul speaks of the fulfillment of those promises in Romans 11:25-29:

> For I would not, brethren, that ye should be ignorant of this mystery, lest ye should be wise in your own conceits; that blindness in part is happened to Israel, until the fullness of the Gentiles be come in. And so all Israel shall be saved: as it is written, There shall come out of Zion the Deliverer, and shall turn away ungodliness from Jacob: For this is my covenant unto them, when I shall take away their sins. As concerning the gospel, they are enemies for your sakes: but as touching the election, they are beloved for the fathers' sakes. For the gifts and calling of God are without repentance.

What Paul is saying here in Romans 11 is that, during the present Church Age, Israel has been judicially blinded but only "in part." Romans 11:7, 8 states:

> What then? Israel hath not obtained that which he seeketh for; but the election hath obtained it, and the rest were blinded (According as it is written, God hath given them the spirit of slumber, eyes that they should not see, and ears that they should not hear;) unto this day.

Only some of the "branches" of Israel have been broken off, and this so that some Gentiles might be "grafted in." We read of this in Romans 11:17-19:

And if some of the branches (Jews) be broken off, and thou (Gentiles), being a wild olive tree, were grafted in among them, and with them partakes of the root and fatness of the olive tree; Boast not against the branches. But if thou boast, thou bearest not the root, but the root thee. Thou wilt say then, The branches were broken off, that I might be grafted in.

Throughout the Church Age, there has been "a remnant (of saved Jews) according to the election of grace" (11:5). Many Christian leaders down through the ages, beginning with the apostles, have been Jews. However, God's primary purpose in the Church Age has been ". . . visiting the Gentiles (nations), to take out of them a people for his name" (Acts 15:14). At the second coming of Christ, "the times of the Gentiles" will end (Luke 21:24) and God will begin again to deal with Israel as His elect nation. The complete restoration of a believing remnant of Israel will climax the purging trials of "the time of Jacob's trouble" (Jer 30:7). This will take place when Christ returns to earth to establish His millennial kingdom centered in Jerusalem (Zech 12:8-10; 13:1; 14:9) following the Great Tribulation. The surviving, repentant, and regenerated Jews will then acknowledge Jesus Christ as their Messiah and Savior in that day.

At the time of Christ's second coming, His subsequent appearance to the remnant of Israel, and her repentance, then Hosea 2:23 will come to fulfillment: "And I will sow her unto me in the earth; and I will have mercy upon her that had not obtained mercy; and I will say to them which were not my people, Thou art my people, and they shall say, Thou art my God."

Because of Israel's rejection of Jesus Christ at His first coming, they have, as a nation, been set aside in unbelief and the gospel has been sent to the Gentiles. This is articulated in Acts 28:25-28:

And when they (the Jewish leaders in Rome) agreed not among themselves, they departed, after that Paul had spoken one word, Well spake the Holy Ghost by Esaias the prophet unto our fathers, Saving, 'Go unto this people, and say Hearing ye shall hear, and shall not understand; and seeing ye shall see, and not perceive: For the heart of this people is waxed gross, and their ears are dull of hearing, and their eyes have they closed; let they should see with their eyes, and hear with their ears, and understand with *their* heart and should be converted, and I should heal them. Be it known therefore unto you, that the salvation of God is sent unto the Gentiles, and *that* they will hear it.

Certainly, individual Jews have come to faith in Christ throughout the Church Age but, as a nation, the Scripture states that they are "not my people" (Hos 2:23). This is certainly borne out in the nation of Israel today, as less than one percent of the Jews in Israel are Christians. There are approximately twenty thousand Messianic Jews in Israel today, a very small percentage of the approximately six million Jews living in Israel today.

Zechariah 13:1, 2 not only promises internal cleansing—morally and spiritually—but also external cleansing, as the country is purged of idols and false prophets, both of which were a constant snare to Israel in the Old Testament. Zechariah speaks of that idolatry in 10:2, 3:

For the idols have spoken vanity, and the diviners have seen a lie, and have told false dreams; they comfort in vain: therefore they went their way as a flock, they were troubled, because there was no shepherd. Mine anger was kindled against the shepherds, and I punished the goats; for the LORD of hosts hath visited his flock the house of Judah, and hath made them as his goodly horse in the battle.

That both idolatry and false prophecy would once again be a problem for Israel in the future is evident not only here but also in Revelation 9:20:

And the rest of the men which were not killed by these plagues yet repented not of the works of their hand, that they should not worship devils, and idols of gold, and silver, and brass, and stone, and of wood: which neither can see, not hear, nor walk.

The "sin of impurity" that inspired the false prophets to lie will also be removed. In that future day if anyone dares to utter false prophecies, his own parent will take the lead in executing him. We see this in Zechariah 13:3:

And it shall come to pass, that when any shall yet prophecy, then his father and his mother that begat him shall say unto him, Thou shalt not live; for thou speakest lies in the name of the LORD: and his father and his mother that begat him shall thrust him through when he prophesieth.

ISRAEL'S MATERIAL RESTORATION

Along with the promise of spiritual restoration for Israel is the assurance of material prosperity. This is revealed in Zechariah 3:9, 10. Keep in mind as you read these verses that, typically, the vine represents Israel's spiritual privileges, and the fig speaks of its national prominence and prosperity.

For behold the stone that I have laid before Joshua; upon one stone shall be seven eyes: behold, I will engrave the graving thereof saith the LORD of hosts, and I will remove the iniquity of that land in one day. In that day saith the LORD of hosts, shall ye call every man his neighbor, under the vine and under the fig tree.

The "stone" must speak of Christ, the "tried stone," the "headstone of the corner" (Psalms 118:22; Isaiah 28:16). The "seven eyes" on the stone would thus indicate, through the perfect number seven, the omniscience and omnipresence of the Messiah. He is also the "Lamb as it had been slain, having seven horns and seven eyes, which are the seven Spirits of God sent forth into all the earth" (Rev 5:6). On this basis alone, that of Christ being "the headstone of the corner," can iniquities be removed.

To the Jews at His first advent, Christ was the stumbling stone and rock of offense (Isa 8:13-15; Matt 21:42; 1 Pet 2:7, 8). But to those who trusted in Him, He was a never-failing refuge (Matt 21:42). Moreover, He is to be the smiting stone to the nations as recorded in Daniel 2:35: ". . . and the stone that smote the image became a great mountain, and filled the whole earth." At present He is the foundation and chief cornerstone of the church (Eph 2:19-22). To the restored nation of Israel in the millennium, He will be the dependable stone of the trusting heart.

REBUILDING AND REIGNING FROM THE TEMPLE

Another activity mentioned in connection with Christ's second coming is His reestablishment of the temple of God. Not only will He reestab-

lish the temple of God, but He will also serve as its High Priest. We see this glorious fact in Zechariah 6:12, 13:

And speak unto him, saying, Thus speaketh the LORD of hosts, saying, Behold the man whose name is the BRANCH; and he shall grow up out of his place, and he shall build the temple of the LORD. Even he shall build the temple of the LORD; and he shall bear the glory, and shall sit and rule upon his throne; and he shall be a priest upon his throne: and the counsel of peace shall be between them both.

Confirming the prophecy of Jeremiah 33:15-17, "the man whose name is the BRANCH," will come to occupy David's throne and to build the millennial temple. Since the rebuilding of the post-exilic temple is to be completed by Zerubbabel (4:9-10), it is difficult to see how this could refer to that temple. Instead, it must be the temple of the Messianic Age. We read concerning this temple in Isaiah 2:2-4:

And it shall come to pass in the last days that the mountains of the LORD's house shall be established in the top of the mountains, and shall be exalted above the hills; and all the nations shall flow unto it. And many people shall go and say, Come ye, and let us go up to the mountain of the LORD, to the house of the God of Jacob; and he will teach us of his ways and we will walk in his paths: for out of Zion shall go forth the law, and the word of the LORD from Jerusalem. And he shall judge among the nations, and shall rebuke many people, and they shall beat their swords into plowshares, their spears into pruninghooks: nation will not lift up sword against nation, neither shall they learn war any more.

In this passage, mountains are symbolic of kings. In the coming Kingdom Age, the Lord will be acknowledged as King over all the earth (Isa 9:6, 7), with His throne at Jerusalem. Not only will Christ be King over all the earth, but He will also be "a priest forever," our eternal Priest-King. Psalm 110:4 speaks of this: "The LORD hath sworn, and will not repent, Thou art a priest for ever after the order of Melchizedek."

Joshua will build the post-exilic temple, along with Zerubbabel, and this becomes a type of Christ as both Priest and King. A full description of this temple is provided in Ezekiel 40-43. It is from this temple in Jerusalem that Christ will serve both as High Priest of the earth and it's Sovereign Leader of government. This will be a time of tremendous rejoicing for the Jews, as they see their great national destiny come to fulfillment. They will be a restored nation, "greater Israel," possessing their promised territory (Gen 15:18; 49:1-28), serving as the center of the worldwide theocratic government, as well as the dwelling place of Christ the Messiah.

WORLDWIDE WORSHIP GIVEN TO REIGNING MESSIAH

Zechariah also predicts that, during the millennium, Jerusalem will be the central location for worship that will be given to Christ as the

reigning Messiah. All nations will make their annual pilgrimage to worship Christ the King! This is unveiled in Zechariah 8:3-8:

This saith the Lord; I am returned unto Zion, and will dwell in the midst of Jerusalem; and Jerusalem shall be called a city of truth, and the mountain of the Lord of hosts, the holy mountain. Thus saith the Lord of hosts; There shall yet old men and old women dwell in the streets of Jerusalem, and every man with his staff in his hand for very age. And the streets of the city shall be full of boys and girls playing in the streets thereof. Thus saith the LORD of hosts; if it be marvelous in the eyes of the remnant of this people in these days, should it be marvelous in mine eyes? Thus saith the LORD of hosts: Behold, I will save my people from the east country, and from the west country; and I will bring them, and they shall dwell in the midst of Jerusalem; and they shall be my people, and I will be their God, in truth and in righteousness.

The name "Jerusalem" means "City of Peace" or "Foundation of Peace." Ironically, more wars have been fought over this city than any other in history. In its more than 5,000 years or inhabited history, it has been anything but the "City of Peace." During its long history Jerusalem has been destroyed twice, once by the Babylonians in 586 B.C., and again by the Romans in A.D. 70. It has been besieged 23 times, attacked 52 times, and captured and recaptured 44 TIMES. It is one of the ironies of history that a city, which in all its long history has seen so little peace and for whose possession such rivers of blood has been shed, should be known as the "City of Peace." In the coming millennium, it will also be the "City of Truth," but only when He who is "the Truth" (John 14:6) is dwelling there. Man's original longevity will be restored in the coming Kingdom Age, when the Lord Jesus "will dwell in the midst of Jerusalem" (8:3). "There shall be no more thence an infant of days nor an old man that not filled his days; for the child shall die an hundred years old. . ." (Isa 65:20).

In addition to restored longevity, the idyllic environmental and political conditions that will prevail during the millennium will enable the population to multiply so rapidly that the people will become "as the sand of the sea" (Rev 20:8) by the end of that thousand-year age. When God promises to "save my people from the east country and from the west country" (Zech 3:7), He is referring to a worldwide regathering from exile, bondage, and dispersion. The promise here is larger than has yet been fulfilled. The regathering of the Jews to Israel during the Church Age is just the beginning of the regathering of Jews to Israel, a process which will be completed subsequent to the Lord's second coming. In Zechariah 8:8, Israel's predicted complete restoration to covenant favor and blessing rests on nothing less than the faithfulness, veracity and righteousness of God:

> And I will bring them, and they shall dwell in the midst of Jerusalem: and they shall be my people, and I will be their God, in truth and in righteousness.

The phrase, ". . . they shall be my people, and I will be their God . . ." is covenant terminology, pertaining to intimate fellowship in a covenant relationship (cf. Gen 17:7, 8; Exod 6:7). Although ethnic Israel is presently going through a Lo-Ammi ("not My people") stage, she will be fully restored as Ammi ("My people"). Quoting from Hosea 2:23; 1:10, and Isaiah 20:22, 23, this is what Paul says of Israel in Romans 9:25-27:

> As he saith also in Osee [Hosea], I will call them my people, which were not my people; and her beloved, which was not beloved. And it shall come to pass, that in the place where it was said unto them, Ye are not my people, they shall be called the children of the living God. Esaiah also crieth concerning Israel, Though the number of the children of Israel be as the sand of the sea, a remnant shall be saved.

It is the book of Zechariah that gives the details as to the time and place where this remnant of Israel will be saved and will once again become "God's people." Let's consider these predictions in Zechariah 12:10; 13:8:

> And I will pour upon the house of David, and upon the inhabitants of Jerusalem, the spirit of grace and of supplications: and they shall look upon me whom they have pierced, and they shall mourn for him, as one mourneth for *his* only *son*, and shall be in bitterness for him, as one that is in bitterness for *his* firstborn . . . And it shall come to pass, *that* in all the land, saith the LORD, two parts therein shall be cut off and die; but the third shall be left therein.

We are told in these passages about the day of national atonement when the one-third remnant of Israel would look upon Christ and recognize Him as they Messiah that they had crucified.

WORLDWIDE PILGRIMAGE TO JERUSALEM

The nations of the world, which throughout history have scorned and persecuted the Jews and ravaged their homeland, shall pay homage and make yearly pilgrimages to Jerusalem, for this is the dwelling place of the Most High God. This turnabout of domination is predicted in Zechariah 14:16-18:

> And it shall come to pass that every one that is left of all the nations which came against Jerusalem shall even go up from year to year to worship the King, the Lord of hosts, and to keep the feast of tabernacles. And it shall be that whoever will not come up of all the families of the earth unto Jerusalem to worship the King, the Lord of hosts, even upon them shall be no rain. And if the family of Egypt go not up, and come not, that have no rain, there shall be the plague, with which the Lord will smite the nations that come not up to keep the feast of the tabernacles.

In spite of the awful decimation predicted in Zechariah 14:12-15, there will be "survivors," a converted remnant from those nations, who will make an annual pilgrimage to Jerusalem "to worship the King." The Feast of Tabernacles was to be a time of grateful rejoicing (Lev 23:40) when the people were to live in "booths" as a reminder that their ancestors lived in booths when the Lord brought them out of Egypt. The festival, as celebrated during the millennium, seems to speak of the final, joyful regathering and restoration of Israel in full kingdom blessing, as well as of the ingathering of the nations.

The prophet here unfolds what will happen to the recalcitrant nations that refuse to send delegations on this annual pilgrimage to worship the King in Jerusalem. The blessing of rain will be withheld from them. According to Deuteronomy 28:22-24, this was one of the curses for covenant disobedience. While in Zechariah the use of rain is literal, it does not exclude the spiritual connotation. In addition to lack of rain, there is the promise of a plague befalling the disobedient nations. As Egypt had experienced plagues at the time of the exodus and through them had been brought to acknowledge God's sovereignty, so plagues were a fitting symbol of disaster in the millennium. Thus will all be punished who do not make the annual pilgrimage to Jerusalem to worship the King and to observe the thankful expressions associated with the Feast of Tabernacles.

WORLDWIDE REJOICING

The book of Zechariah concludes on a note of worldwide rejoicing, as Israel and the rest of the nations are brought into joyful submission to the global reign of the Messiah, the Lord Jesus Christ. This is the true NEW WORLD ORDER, as opposed to the "New World Order" (which is merely a technocratic version of the "Old World Order" of feudal tyranny) that the devil's crowd is trying to impose on humanity in this present age. This note of rejoicing is sounded in Zechariah 14:20, 21:

> In that day shall there be upon the bells of the horses, HOLINESS UNTO THE LORD; and the pots in the LORD's house shall be like the bowls before the altar. Yes, every pot in Jerusalem and in Judah shall be holiness unto the

LORD of hosts, and all they that sacrifice shall come and take of them, and seethe therein: and in that day there shall be no more the Canaanite in the house of the LORD of hosts.

In these final verses of Zechariah, the nature of the Messianic kingdom is depicted: it will be characterized by "holiness." This holiness will be so pervasive that every common vessel throughout the city and the whole land shall be so holy that it would be fitting even for service in the sanctuary, and every profane person will be forever banished from the house of the Lord. All distinctions between sacred and secular shall be at an end, because all shall now be alike *holy*. The teaching of these verses may be summed up like this: There will be holiness in public life ("the bells of the horses," vs. 20), in religious life ("the cooking pots in the Lord's house," vs 20), and in private life ("every pot in Jerusalem and Judah," vs. 20). Even common things become holy when they are used in God's service.

"Holy to the LORD" was engraved on the plate of gold worn on the turban of the high priest (Exod 19:6). Finally, in the Messianic era, God's original purpose for Israel will be fulfilled. Israel will be a holy nation when ". . . the Holy One of Israel is our king" (Psalm 89:18). This final scene of the book of Zechariah reveals that it is much more than just a history book. It is a book that is sprinkled with detailed prophecies of our Lord's first coming and brimming with prophecies concerning His glorious second coming and worldwide reign as mankind's Priest and King. Zechariah is truly a fantastic book of specific and detailed prophecy regarding the first and second comings of Christ.

Just as we have seen the literal fulfillment of all that which pertains to Christ in His first coming as the suffering Savior, so also can we expect and anticipate that there will be literal fulfillment in the time ahead of that which pertains to Christ in His second coming as the glorious King. Zechariah truly holds the key to interpreting Bible prophecy!

An appropriate response to all of these glorious truths is to echo Robert Grant's exhortation:

O worship the King, all-glorious above,
And gratefully sing His pow'r and His love;
Our Shield and Defender the Ancient of days,
Pavilioned in splendor and girded with praise.

RECOMMENDED READING

Anderson, Sir Robert. *The Coming Prince*. Grand Rapids: Kregel Publications, 19th ed., 1975 (originally published in 1894).

Gaebelein, Arno. *Studies in Zechariah*. NY: Francis Fitch, Inc., 8th ed., 1956 (originally published in 1911).

Larkin, Clarence. *Dispensational Truth*. NY: Cosimo Classics, 2008 (originally published in 1920).

Levy, David. *Zechariah: Israel's Prophetic Future and the Coming Apocalypse*. Bellmawr, NJ: The Friends of Israel Gospel Ministry, Inc., 2011.

Neutzling, Michael. *The Devil is Coming in 3-D, A Commentary on the Book of Zechariah*. Fig Tree Press, Undated.

93123243R00079

Made in the USA
Columbia, SC
05 April 2018